Employment law for the construction industry

second edition

Michael Ryley and **Edward Goodwyn**

Published by Thomas Telford Publishing, Thomas Telford Ltd, 1 Heron Quay, London E14 4JD.
www.thomastelford.com

Distributors for Thomas Telford books are
USA: ASCE Press, 1801 Alexander Bell Drive, Reston, VA 20191-4400
Japan: Maruzen Co. Ltd, Book Department, 3–10 Nihonbashi 2-chome, Chuo-ku, Tokyo 103
Australia: DA Books and Journals, 648 Whitehorse Road, Mitcham 3132, Victoria

First edition published 2000
Second edition published 2008

Also available from Thomas Telford Books
Construction Law Handbook 2008 edition. Eds Sir Vivial Ramsey QC *et al.*
ISBN 978-0-7277-3567-6
Engineers' Dispute Resolution Handbook. Ed. R. Gaitskell. ISBN 978-0-7277-3450-1
Quantifying and Managing Disruption Claims. H. Lal. ISBN 978-0-7277-3165-3

A catalogue record for this book is available from the British Library

ISBN: 978-0-7277-3460-0

© Michael Ryley and Edward Goodwyn 2008

Typeset by Academic + Technical, Bristol
Index created by Indexing Specialists (UK) Ltd, Hove, East Sussex
Printed and bound in Great Britain by MPG Books, Bodmin, Cornwall

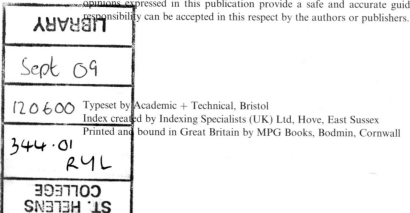

Contents

Preface

The management of employment law issues has always been an important part of running any construction project. As employee rights are extended and as regulation increases, the significance of these issues is growing continually.

Employment Law for the Construction Industry has been written as a guide for those working in the construction industry who have to deal with day-to-day employment issues and who need to be able to access quick, easy and practical advice. A multitude of general works has already been written which explain the principles of employment law, and it is not our intention to add another. Our approach starts from the perspective that the range of employment issues specific to the construction industry, in which some 10% of the UK workforce is employed, justifies a book devoted to them alone. We have therefore confined ourselves to a discussion of the employment law issues that are of particular significance for the construction industry. In order to achieve our objective of keeping the book at a manageable length, we have had to omit coverage of many of the general employment law issues that are not specific to the industry, but which the employer in the construction industry may nevertheless be expected to come across.

This second edition of the book is fully revised in order to take account of the many changes since the first edition was written in 2000: not least the 2006 revision of TUPE, the changes to the Construction Industry Scheme and the developments in the area of employment status.

In an attempt to make the book more easily readable, we have endeavoured to keep the text free of references and citations. For those who would like to explore the issues covered by the book in greater detail, the bibliography contains suggestions for further reading.

The law is stated as at February 1st 2008.

About the authors

Michael Ryley

Michael Ryley is a partner in the Employment Group at Pinsent Masons, based in the London office. He was educated at Bolton School and St John's College, Oxford. With the exception of a secondment to a firm of lawyers in Tokyo, he has spent his career to date in central London, advising clients on all aspects of employment law and HR strategy.

Although he advises clients in relation to employment litigation, Michael spends the bulk of his time advising on the commercial aspects of employment law. He has a long-standing interest in the impact of business transfers on employees, a subject on which he has spoken and written extensively. Michael has considerable experience of acquisitions and disposals, both in the UK and internationally. With the growth of public and private sector outsourcing, Michael has become involved in many cases acting for both clients and contractors, advising on TUPE and its implications. Michael advises a number of construction companies in relation to HR strategy, boardroom disputes, the employment aspects of infrastructure projects, and individual and collective dispute resolution. He has been involved in a number of major projects including the construction of Wembley Stadium and the construction of the 2012 site.

Michael is a regular speaker at and chairman of seminars on employment law topics. He is the author of *Employment Law Aspects of Mergers and Acquisitions – a Practical Guide*, *Employment Law and Information Technology*, *TUPE: Law and Practice* (with Professor Robert Upex) and many articles on employment law, particularly on the impact of TUPE on business transfers.

Edward Goodwyn

Edward is a partner in the Employment Group in Pinsent Masons' London office. He was educated at Wellington College and Exeter University. Having joined Masons in 1992 as a trainee solicitor, Edward qualified as a solicitor in 1994. He has specialised exclusively in employment law since qualification.

Edward has principally been engaged in advising corporate and public sector clients on all aspects of employment law, both contentious and non-contentious. He advises a large number of construction companies, contractors and sub-contractors alike on HR issues, including ones such as the pressure on industry to move away from self-employment status, the on-going skills shortage, interpretation of the industry's collective agreements and the CIS. He is also experienced in advising on specialist TUPE-related transactional work on major projects and outsourcing both in the private and public sectors. His advice has included the drafting of company handbooks, HR policies, employment contracts, and the protection of confidential information and customer contracts.

On the contentious side, Edward has represented a number of construction companies in the Employment Tribunals, Employment Appeal Tribunal, High Court and Court of Appeal in relation to all aspects of employment disputes. This has included defending claims for unfair and wrongful dismissal, TUPE-related claims, equal pay, injunctive proceedings, disability, race and sex discrimination claims, and more recently claims brought under the Working Time Regulations, the Public Interest Disclosure Act and Age Discrimination Regulations.

Edward is a regular contributor to *Construction News* and *Building*, and has written and presented numerous seminars and up-dates on many aspects of employment law. He is a member of the Employment Lawyers' Association.

Abbreviations

ACS	Accredited Certification Scheme
AEEU	Amalgamated Engineering and Electrical Union
B&CE	Building and Civil Engineering Group
B&CEJB	Building and Civil Engineering Joint Board
BERR	Department for Business, Enterprise and Regulatory Reform
CAC	Central Arbitration Committee
CAS	Construction Apprentice Scheme
CIS	Construction Industry Scheme
CECCB	Civil Engineering Construction Conciliation Board
CIJC	Construction Industry Joint Council
CITB	Construction Industry Training Board
CORGI	Council for Registered Gas Installers
COSOP	Cabinet Office Statement of Practice
CRE	Commission for Racial Equality (now the Equality and Human Rights Commission)
CSCS	Construction Skills Certification Scheme
DTI	Department for Trade and Industry
EAT	Employment Appeal Tribunal
ECITB	Engineering Construction Industry Training Board
EEA	European Economic Area
ERA	Employment Rights Act 1996
ETO	Economic Technical or Organisational
FCEC	Federation of Civil Engineering Contractors
GMB	General Municipal Boilermakers' and Allied Trades Union
HMRC	Her Majesty's Revenue and Customs
HVAC	Heating, Ventilating, Air Conditioning, Piping and Domestic Engineering Industry

HVCA	Heating and Ventilating Contractors' Association
JIB	Joint Industry Board
MEP	Member of the European Parliament
MSF	Manufacturing Science Finance
NAECI	National Agreement for the Engineering Construction Industry
NHS	National Health Service
NIC	National Insurance Contributions
NJC	National Joint Council
NJCBI	National Joint Council for the Building Industry
NJIC	National Joint Industrial Council
NMW	National Minimum Wage
NVQ	National Vocational Qualification
PAYE	Pay as You Earn
PFI	Private Finance Initiative
PJC	Project Joint Council
PPP	Public Private Partnerships
RPI	Retail Price Index
SSP	Statutory Sick Pay
SVQ	Scottish Vocational Qualification
TGWU	Transport and General Workers' Union
TUPE	Transfer of Undertakings (Protection of Employment) Regulations 2006
UCATT	Union of Construction, Allied Trades and Technicians
VAT	Value Added Tax

CHAPTER 1

The structure of the employment relationship

Recent years have seen a marked change in the pattern of employment within the construction industry. Particularly significant has been the decision of HM Revenue and Customs[1] to focus on the industry, which has resulted in a considerable increase in the number of workers classified as 'employees'. As a consequence, a greater proportion of the industry's workforce is now covered by the employment protection laws and the degree of regulation of the working relationship has increased as a result. Additionally, the period from the latter part of the 1990s into the twenty-first century has been notable for the enactment of a considerable amount of employment related legislation. Most notable have been changes in the law at European Union (EU) level, driven by developing social policy, and these, together with changes made at Westminster, have provided workers in the industry with enhanced rights. As a result the industry has been compelled to rise to the challenge of managing a workforce whilst being subject to greater obligations and at the same time seeking to operate in a cost effective way within the industry's tight margins.

Until the introduction of the Construction Industry Tax Deduction Scheme (the 714 Scheme) in 1972, the industry had engaged its workforce on a largely transient basis. The fluctuating demand for labour in the lifecycle of a typical construction project and the nomadic nature of workers led to an industry which promoted 'casualisation'. The 714 Scheme introduced a degree of regulation in respect of workers on 'the lump', almost exclusively for tax collection purposes, and allowed a large part of the industry's workforce to remain transient and self-employed. However, in 1996 the industry had to reassess the way it engaged its workforce as a result of the Inland Revenue/Contributions Agency 'clamp-down'. The final pieces in the clamp-down were put in place with the Construction Industry Scheme (CIS)[2] which took effect on 1 August 1999.[3] The importance of this reclassification of the industry's workforce, whereby a substantially increased number of employees are now on construction companies' books, cannot be underestimated. Amongst its effects on construction companies have been the following:

- Companies have experienced a substantial increase in Class 1 Employer's National Insurance Contributions.
- There has been an increase in construction companies' obligations to their workforces in that workers who are classified as employees are now entitled to more extensive rights than they were when self-employed. For example, employees enjoy the following rights which would not apply to the self-employed:
  (a) redundancy payments and the right not to be unfairly dismissed;
  (b) paid holiday under the Working Time Regulations 1998;
  (c) the minimum wage;
  (d) Statutory Sick and Maternity Pay;
  (e) protection from unlawful deductions from their pay.
  These additional employment rights have added to construction companies' labour costs and have increased the importance of effective human resources management (HRM).
- Companies have lost some of their ability to be flexible in reacting to market pressures in their use of a transient workforce, as a greater proportion of the workforce is now committed to a sole employer.
- On the positive side, companies have gained some protection in terms of securing their workforce in the event of a skill shortage in the labour market. By placing their workers on their books as employees, companies have been able to increase training opportunities and employee retention by building up goodwill and by providing incentives to longer-term employment such as pension scheme membership. Certain construction companies have led the way in using this approach to acquire a competitive advantage in the labour market.

1.1. SOURCES OF EMPLOYMENT LAW WITHIN THE INDUSTRY

The rights and obligations of employees derive from five principal sources:

- individual contracts;
- statutory rights and obligations;

- collective agreements;
- collective bargaining and trade union recognition;
- European law.

1.1.1. Individual contracts

It is often assumed by employers that when an employee does not have a written contract of employment, the employer is not bound by any obligations to the employee. This is not the case. A court is likely to identify a contract of employment from the fact that a 'wage/work bargain' has been agreed between employer and employee. Contracts may be oral or written. Where contracts are silent on any given term of employment a court may be prepared to imply a term. For example, where a contract is silent on the length of notice required to terminate the contract, a court will generally imply a term to the effect that the contract is terminable upon reasonable notice and will evaluate what is reasonable in each case against the background of industry norms.

Where there appears at first sight to be no written contract at all, a court may be prepared to identify a contract from the existence of a relationship whereby work is undertaken in exchange for payment, deriving the terms of that contract largely from how the relationship operates in practice. Terms may also be derived from custom and practice, where the habitual practice of the employer gives rise to a reasonable expectation on the part of employees that the employer will follow a similar practice in future. For example, where an employee with no written contract has received overtime payments at double time for working on site on Sundays, he could expect a court to imply such a term to force his employer to make similar double-time payments in the future.

Additionally, the courts recognise that certain terms are essential to the relationship of employer and employee, regardless of whether these have been the subject of express agreement in the employment contract. These include duties on the part of the employee of:

- fidelity;
- obedience;
- working with due diligence and care; and
- trust and confidence;

and duties on the part of the employer:

- of trust and confidence; and
- to provide a safe place of work/safe system of work.

Under English law there is no obligation for a contract of employment to be reduced to writing. However, certainty is greatly assisted by doing so. Moreover, there is a statutory obligation on an employer to provide an employee with a written statement of certain terms and conditions of

> **Statutory written particulars of employment**
> The following particulars must be given to all employees in writing no later than two months from the employee's start of employment:
>
> - name of employee
> - name of employer
> - job title or description
> - commencement date of employment
> - commencement date of continuous employment
> - details of pay with method and frequency of payment
> - hours of work
> - place of work or, if mobile, the employer's address
> - sickness or injury terms, including sick pay
> - pension terms and conditions and whether a contracting-out certificate is in force
> - period of notice
> - holiday entitlements and holiday pay
> - reference to grievance and disciplinary procedures
> - particulars of any applicable collective agreement that directly affect the terms and conditions of employment
> - details of work, pay, length of time for work outside the UK
> - if the job is not permanent, an indication of when it will end.

employment not later than two months after the beginning of the employment.[4] The terms which must be included are set out in the accompanying box.

Chapter 3 contains examples of pro forma written particulars prepared for employees whose terms and conditions are determined by two of the industry's main collective agreements.

It is apparent that there are many rights and obligations which might be expected to arise in connection with the employment relationship, which fall outside the scope of the statutory statement of written particulars, especially those terms and conditions which are likely to be of benefit to the employer. Employers are well advised to provide their employees with written contracts which incorporate those terms which must be set out in writing to comply with the statutory minimum, but which also contain a more comprehensive set of terms and conditions, taking the opportunity to build in appropriate rights and protections.

1.1.2. Statutory rights and obligations

These include Acts of Parliament and Statutory Instruments which regulate the employment contract, often superseding contractual rights. For example, employees may acquire the right to receive a redundancy payment regardless of the fact that no such provision is made in the contract agreed between the employer and the employee. Notwithstanding that the employer and the employee have agreed a short notice period to reflect both parties' desire not to be bound to the other after completion on any particular site, this may be overridden by the statutory minimum period of notice. Increasingly, statutory regulation of the employment relationship is eroding the freedom of employers and employees to negotiate whatever terms of employment they wish. One of the most notable examples is the National Minimum Wage Act 1998, which came into force in April 1999. Whilst the majority of workers in the industry are paid over the minimum wage (the principal rate of which is currently £5.52 per hour) due to the minimum pay rates collectively agreed through the various working rule agreements, the legislation will be relevant in some sectors where employers will have to ensure that their labourers, for example, are paid at or over the minimum wage. The minimum wage is subject to increases over time in accordance with reviews by the Low Pay Commission.

The rights and obligations conferred by these various pieces of legislation depend, in many cases, on the status of the worker. The legislation is some-what inconsistent as to whether rights and obligations are conferred on 'employees', those who operate under a 'contract of service', 'workers', those who 'undertake personal services' or those 'in business on their own account'. For these purposes, the assessment of whether a brickie who has been working on site for six months until completion is an employee, in business on his own account, or a worker undertaking personal services, is extremely difficult and yet is crucial to understanding the rights which he has and the duties owed to him. In general, rights conferred by the relevant legislation will always apply to employees and, to a much lesser extent, non-employees. Although the coverage of statutory rights is increasingly being extended to a broader category of workers, the distinction between who is and who is not an employee is nevertheless of fundamental importance to the industry. It is explored in detail in Chapter 2.

1.1.3. Collective agreements

Terms and conditions may be agreed on a collective basis whereby the representatives of a group of employees (which may be defined by refer-ence to their skills or their employer) meet to reach agreement with their employers. Many employers within the industry adhere to standard terms and conditions of employment, which are the product of national-level collective bargaining between employers' representatives and officials of recognised trade unions. These terms regulate each individual employ-ment relationship within the scope of the collective agreement; in practice they operate as a standard form employment contract.

The main collective agreements that relate to the industry[5] are discussed in Chapter 3. In many cases, wage rates and the terms and conditions of employment of workers in the industry are determined by these collective agreements. An employer's obligation to provide a written statement of terms and conditions of employment is satisfied by the employer referring the employee to the collective agreement which directly affects his terms and conditions, so long as the employee has a reasonable opportunity of reading the collective agreement in the course of his employment or it has been otherwise made reasonably accessible to him in some other way. Nevertheless, it is common practice for the employee to be provided with a conventional statement of terms and conditions, some examples of which are contained in Chapter 3.

Ordinarily, a collective agreement will establish the 'norm' or standard for the terms and conditions of employment for workers within its scope. However, a collective agreement does not automatically bind or benefit an individual employee. The mere fact that an employee is a member of, say, UCATT (Union of Construction, Allied Trades and Technicians), which may have been involved in the negotiation of a collective agreement which governs employees of a description into which the employee falls, does not give that employee an automatic right to benefit from the collective agreement. A route must be found whereby it can be said that the employer and the employee have elected that the employment be governed by the collective agreement. The terms of the industry's collective agreements may be incorporated into individual contracts of employment either through an express provision of incorporation contained in the employee's contract or through an implied term incorporating the agreement as a matter of custom and practice. In either case, the collective agreement will be incorporated notwithstanding that the particular employee may not approve of all the details which the unions have negotiated or may not even be a member of one of the relevant unions.

Generally, once the terms of a collective agreement are incorporated into an individual's contract, the relevant contractual terms are unaffected by the termination of the collective agreement. This issue has been very much in evidence following the demise of the Federation of Civil Engineering Contractors and the effect it had on the old CECCB (Civil Engineering Construction Conciliation Board) Working Rule Agreement, the Federation being one of the parties to the bargaining progress. As a matter of law, the old CECCB Working Rule Agreement could no longer be validly negotiated each year by reason of the fact that one of the parties to the Agreement had ceased to exist. Employees with the CECCB Working Rule Agreement incorporated into their contracts of employment effectively had their terms frozen. Only by either agreeing to enter into another form of collective bargaining and working rule agreement, such as the Construction Industry Joint Council Working Rule Agreement, or by negotiating locally, could their terms and conditions be changed. Similarly, it will be a question of interpretation as to whether the true construction of an employment contract is that it incorporates the collective agreement which is for the time being in force. In such a case, agreed variations in the collective agreement at national level may be ineffective to alter the terms of the individual contract of employment. In the case of the industry's collective agreements, because pay rates are negotiated on an annual basis, it is usual to find that the collective agreement that is incorporated into individual contracts of employment is the one currently in force.

It must always be remembered that an employee can choose to negotiate his terms and conditions of employment with his employer on an individual basis rather than collectively. Just how feasible this is in practice will depend on local circumstances. It is the parties' (i.e. the employee's and the employer's) intentions that are critical in determining whether a collective agreement is to be incorporated.[6]

1.1.4. Collective bargaining and trade union recognition

The right of recognition for trade unions is a highly political subject and the law in this area has varied depending on which political party is in power. The Labour Government under the leadership of Tony Blair pledged to reintroduce the compulsory recognition of trade unions and provisions to this effect came into force in the summer of 2000.

As a consequence, employers in the industry with more than 20 workers who do not voluntarily recognise unions such as UCATT, GMB or Unite may have a duty imposed upon them to recognise and to engage in collective bargaining.[7] The scope of mandatory bargaining includes pay, hours and holidays. Where there is a dispute concerning recognition, the Central Arbitration Committee (CAC) has the power to grant or to deny recognition and to enforce collective bargaining where recognition has been granted. The statutory procedure for recognition provides a voluntary and a compulsory mechanism. The basic principles are set out in Table 1.1.

It is worth noting that there are also statutory procedures for de-recognition, changes to the bargaining unit (battles around how the bargaining unit should be defined are frequent in this area) and for specifying the method of bargaining.

1.1.5. European law

Directives issued by the EU may impact on the employment relationship either directly (in the public sector) or otherwise indirectly in that Member States will be obliged to enact legislation which incorporates the provisions of the directives into national law. Regard must be had to the judgments of the Court of Justice of the European Communities in the interpretation of directives.

Table 1.1. Main issues leading to union recognition

1. Trade union makes formal request for recognition to employer in respect of a particular bargaining unit

2. The employer has ten days to respond to the request. If the request is rejected or ignored the union can apply to the CAC. If the employer is willing to negotiate, an extra 20 days are available in addition to the first ten, for the employer and trade union to conduct negotiations as to the identity of the bargaining unit and mechanisms for collective bargaining (this time limit can be further extended)

3. If the employer refuses to agree or the negotiations break down, the trade union can formally apply to the CAC to act as brokers to decide the appropriate bargaining unit and to decide whether a majority of workers in the bargaining unit support recognition. At this stage, the employer can apply to ACAS for their assistance in any voluntary negotiations, thereby effectively delaying the involvement of the CAC

4. The CAC initially has ten days (which may be extended) to consider the validity of any application and to see whether it is admissible. In order to proceed, an application must, inter alia:
   - be received by the employer;
   - be made by an independent union;
   - relate to an employer with 21 or more workers;
   - be in the proper form;
   - be copied to the employer with any supporting documents;
   - not cover any workers in respect of whom a union is already recognised;
   - satisfy the CAC that at least 10% of the proposed bargaining unit are members of the union and that a majority of the workers is likely to favour recognition;
   - show that the unions will co-operate in collective bargaining; and
   - not be substantially the same as an application which the CAC has accepted within the previous three years

5. If the above threshold test is satisfied, a further 20-day window is provided for the parties to agree the bargaining unit. The CAC may choose to extend this period.

   If no agreement on the bargaining unit is reached, the CAC must determine the bargaining unit within ten working days, taking into account the need for the bargaining unit to be compatible with effective management

6. Once the bargaining unit has been established, the CAC must satisfy itself that the majority of workers in the bargaining unit are members of the union seeking recognition

7. If the above is satisfied, the CAC shall issue a declaration of recognition without a ballot, unless:
   7.1. a 'significant number' of union members tell the CAC they oppose recognition; or
   7.2. the CAC has doubts that a significant number of union members in the bargaining unit want recognition; or
   7.3. the CAC thinks that the interests of good industrial relations require a ballot.
   If so, the matter goes to a secret ballot

8.   The ballot requires the support of a majority of those voting and 40% of those entitled to vote. Twenty days are allowed for the ballot to take place

9.   Granting or rejecting an application settles the issue of recognition for three years

10. Once recognition is granted, CAC has the power to impose legally binding procedures for collective bargaining on the parties if they cannot agree procedures themselves

The social policy of the EU has spawned a considerable amount of legislation in recent years, the impact of which has been felt throughout the construction industry, notably through legislation on working time and on the transfer of undertakings.

The process of enacting legislation in Westminster to implement EU directives has proved problematic. The resulting legislation has often proved difficult to interpret with consequent practical problems for the industry. One of the most notable examples of this is the Transfer of Undertakings (Protection of Employment) Regulations 2006 (TUPE)[8] which are notoriously difficult to apply in practice. For example, a contractor pricing a building's maintenance contract on a re-tender may be unable to predict the employment consequences of winning the tender, including calculating precisely the employment related liabilities he may inherit. The courts have done little to clarify such EU-related legislation, TUPE being a notorious example once again, and where the government has published written guidance in conjunction with the legislation this has often been of limited assistance. Indeed, the guidance initially published in connection with the Working Time Regulations,[9] left as many questions unanswered as it solved and amendment was required as a consequence. As a result, on building sites across the country, a given legal requirement could be interpreted in different ways with no one clear as to which is the definitive position.

NOTES

1. and its predecessors including, prior to its incorporation with the Inland Revenue, the then Contributions Agency of the Department of Social Security
2. Discussed in greater detail in Chapter 4
3. although the Inland Revenue granted transitional arrangements delaying the enforcement of the CIS until 5 November 1999. The scheme was subsequently superseded by the new Construction Industry Scheme. The latter came into force in April 2007, applying to some 200 000 registered contractors and 900 000 subcontractors
4. Section 1, Employment Rights Act 1996 (ERA)
5. the Construction Industry Joint Council Working Rule Agreement, the National Agreement for the Engineering Construction Industry, the National Working Rules of the Joint Industry Board for the Electrical Contracting Industry, the

National Agreement as to Working Rules for Operatives in the Heating, Ventilating, Air Conditioning, Piping and Domestic Engineering Industry and the Joint Industry Board for Plumbing Mechanical Engineering Services in England and Wales

6. *Wall & Others* v. *Standard Telephones & Cables Limited*
7. Schedule 1 Employment Relations Act 1999, now under Schedule A1 Trade Union and Labour Relations (Consolidation) Act 1992, as amended by the Employee Relations Act 2004
8. which are discussed in greater detail in Chapter 9
9. See Chapter 5

CHAPTER 2

The status of the working relationship

In any assessment of rights and obligations in the workplace, the distinction between an 'employee', a 'worker' and someone who is self-employed is of paramount importance. This is a recurrent issue in the construction industry and is therefore explored in some detail in this chapter.

Unfortunately, the distinction is notoriously unclear and, as a result, the determination of the true status of workers has never been easy. In *Stephenson Jordan* v. *Harrison Limited*, Lord Denning remarked:

> It is almost impossible to give a precise definition... It is often easy to recognise a contract of service [employment contract] when you see it but it is difficult to say wherein the difference [between it and self-employed contractor status] lies.

2.1. WHY IS THE DISTINCTION IMPORTANT?

Many employment protection rights are only available to employees – hence defining whether a given worker falls within the scope of these protections is determined by categorising the worker as an employee or otherwise. Moreover, courts will imply into a contract of employment various rights and duties that do not form a part of the relationship with other categories of worker. The distinction is also important in the context of vicarious liability. An employer will ordinarily be responsible for the wrongful acts of his employees in the course of their employment; conversely, a company will not usually be liable for the acts of a contractor, unless it has chosen to do so by contract.

Due to recent legislative changes, the distinction is becoming more and more important, although where the lines are drawn between the different statuses still remains difficult to say. The current government has looked to extend the ambit of employment rights to workers who may not enjoy employment status. The foundations for further expansion of these rights to non-employee workers have already been laid. Buried deep within the Employment Relations Act 1999 at section 23 lies legislation that enables the government to extend coverage of many statutory employment rights to atypical workers by secondary legislation. The enactment of this power under section 23 encouraged the government in July 2002 to introduce the 'Employment Status Review' which proposed to address whether the 'present coverage of employment rights reflects the underlying economic reality of the employment relationship and whether a different coverage would better meet [the government's] aims for the labour market'. The review concluded on 30 March 2006 with the then DTI (Department for Trade and Industry) (now BERR) announcing that there was no need at that stage to extend the employment rights of atypical workers.[1] The government commented that 'we believe changes to the legal framework would not prevent instances of abuse or lack of awareness. It would however damage labour market flexibility and result in a reduction in overall employment'. Nonetheless, we have seen in the last few years a significant rise in the amount of employment legislation drafted particularly to support those who can be described as atypical workers (as opposed to an employee). To illustrate the practical consequences of the distinction, some of the principal rights and obligations of employees, workers and self-employed contractors are contrasted in the accompanying boxes.

Rights of employees
- Statutory compensation rights on termination of work/dismissal
- Right not to be unfairly dismissed (subject to the necessary continuous service)
- Right to a redundancy payment (subject to the necessary continuous service)
- Right to written particulars of employment terms
- Protection from discrimination (sex; race; disability; age; sexual orientation; and religion or belief)
- Minimum periods of notice
- Guarantee payments
- Parental leave

- Right to equal pay for work of equal value
- Maternity rights
- Time off for trade union activities
- Full health and safety rights
- Statutory Sick Pay (SSP)
- Right to be paid wages without unauthorised deductions
- Rights to statutory disciplinary, dismissal and grievance procedures
- In some cases, the right to benefit from collective agreements such as the various industry working rule agreements

Obligations of employees
- To comply with the employer's lawful orders
- To work with due diligence and to work faithfully
- To give the contractually agreed period of notice to terminate the employment
- To pay employment income tax (tax will be withheld by the employer under PAYE)
- To pay Class 1 National Insurance Contributions (NIC) by way of the employer

Rights of 'workers'
- Rights to rest breaks, time off and paid holidays under the Working Time Regulations
- Right to a minimum wage
- Protection from discrimination (sex; race; disability; age; sexual orientation; and religion or belief)
- Right to be paid wages without unauthorised deductions
- To be provided with a safe place and a safe system of work but to a lesser extent than employees

Rights of self-employed contractors
- To benefit only from those entitlements that have been expressly agreed
- To a lesser extent than employees, to be provided with a safe place and safe system of work
- To be paid fees gross, free of deduction

Obligations of workers and contractors
- To comply only with contractual obligations that have been expressly agreed
- To work with skill and diligence
- To pay tax on trading income
- To pay Class 2 and Class 4 self-employed National Insurance Contributions (NIC)

Note also that there is no longer any distinction between the protection afforded to part-time employees and full-time employees. If a worker is truly an employee, the number of hours worked per week is not determinative of the extent of the rights which apply to them.

2.2. EMPLOYEE, WORKER OR CONTRACTOR?

Surprisingly, there is no statutory definition of an 'employee' save for the rather unhelpful definition in s230(1) Employment Rights Act 1996 which states an employee is:

an individual who has entered into a contract of employment.

'Contract of employment' is then defined as:

a contract of service or apprenticeship whether express or implied, and (if it is express) whether oral or in writing.

As a result of these unspecific definitions, it is necessary to turn as a guide to previous judgments of the courts when distinguishing between employees and other workers. Uncertainty concerning the precise extent of the definition of an employee has spawned literally hundreds of cases on this subject. Despite this long history, there is still no definitive test which can be used in all cases to determine whether or not a worker is an employee or a contractor. Moreover, a number of the decisions of the courts appear to conflict. However, more recently, the cases have suggested that there are at least two 'irreducible minima' needed for an employment contract or worker relationship to exist – that of personal service and mutuality of obligation. The nature and extent of the control exercised on the individual then determines whether he is an employee or worker. A more detailed analysis of these cases is considered later in this chapter.

The following practical guidelines are suggested in the light of both the uncertainty as to the exact scope of the term 'employee' and the guidance given in the case law:

- Place all employees and contractors on contracts to formalise the relationship and to reflect the differences in the way in which employees and contractors are engaged.

- The contracts must reflect the parties' intentions and must not be a sham.
- Ensure contractors are entitled to use substitutes to undertake the work as opposed to being contractually obliged to undertake the work personally.
- In contractors' contracts, expressly provide that the employer is under no obligation to provide work and, similarly, that the contractors are under no obligation to accept work.
- Ensure that contractors are not entitled to sick pay, holiday pay, to bring a grievance under any grievance procedure nor are they subject to disciplinary action.
- Ensure and, if possible, record that both the employer's and the contractors' intentions were to enter into a relationship of employer and contractor, not one of employer/employee.
- Pay employees through the payroll but pay the contractors on receipt of an invoice. If possible, do not pay contractors an hourly rate – but a fixed price.
- Place some financial risk on the contractors – either a penalty for late or unsatisfactory work or an incentive if work is completed on time.
- Only provide tools and plant to employees – require contractors to provide their own.
- Whilst contractors are on site, allow them to control how they work as far as possible and reflect this autonomy in their contracts.
- Make sure your contractors take out their own insurance in respect of injury to themselves and liability to third parties.

Over the years the courts have suggested a number of tests to determine employee status. These are explained below and general conclusions are then drawn which explain why the practical guidance given above is suggested.

2.2.1. The 'control test'

Early cases placed great emphasis on the employer's right to exercise control over what, how, when and where a worker was to work. The greater the degree of control, the greater the likelihood that the worker was an employee.

The courts have taken the view that control of itself is insufficient to determine status, particularly where highly skilled workers are involved. Although many manual workers in the industry will be subject to a high degree of control and will clearly be employees, it will often be completely impracticable for an employer to tell a more qualified person how and when to perform his other duties. However, this does not mean that the worker is not an employee.

Control is now seen merely as one of the factors to take into account in determining the question of employment status; an important factor but not one which is determinative. Other factors must be taken into account as well. For example, in one of the leading cases in this area, *Ready-Mixed Concrete (South East) Limited* v. *Minister of Pensions and National Insurance*, Ready-Mixed Concrete exercised a high degree of control over a lorry driver, but the driver was held to be self-employed. He was not required to drive the lorry personally and could arrange for a substitute driver to take his place. This was held to be inconsistent with the status of an employee and consistent with a contractor's status.

2.2.2. The 'integration test'

In many ways this test arose out of the inadequacies of the control test. The question to be asked is whether the worker or the work done forms an integral part of the business to which it is being supplied. It assumes that a contractor is usually engaged for a specific job to provide 'a service', whereas an employee is integrated into the main business of the employer.

The test has been of specific use in reviewing the status of professional and skilled employees. For example, a surgeon, being a highly skilled worker, was not subject to the 'control' of a hospital but the hospital was vicariously liable for his acts because he was an integral part of the hospital organisation and was held to be an employee.[2]

2.2.3. The 'economic reality test'

This test asks whether the worker is in business on his or her own account.

In the leading case of *Market Investigations Limited* v. *Minister of Social Security*, the question was whether market research workers were employees. They were part-time interviewers for a market research organisation producing market surveys. Each survey was carried out for a separate fee. The research workers were free to accept or to reject work, to fix their own hours, and to undertake work for other organisations. They were not subject to direct supervision. They did not get holiday or sick pay. Despite these factors suggesting to the contrary, the court concluded that these workers were in fact employees, because they were not in business on their own account.

A similar conclusion was reached in the Hong Kong case of *Lee Ting Sang* v. *Chung Chie Keung and Shun Shing Construction and Engineering Co. Limited*, which also applied this test. Mr Lee was a stonemason. He was injured in an accident at work and claimed that he was an employee so as to benefit from the contractor's insurance policy. Mr Lee did not provide his own equipment or hire his own helpers. From time to time he worked for other contractors. He prioritised the work of the sub- and main contractor when it was urgent. He had no responsibility for investment or management of the work on the construction site. He did not price the job. He was paid either for piece work or on a daily rate. The court said:

> Taking all the foregoing considerations into account the picture emerges of a skilled artisan earning his living by working for more than one employer as an employee and not a small businessman venturing into business on his own account as an independent contractor with all its attendant risks.

This case confirms that a worker can work for more than one party and be an employee of one or all of them.

2.2.4. The 'multiple test'

The multiple test involves an analysis of a 'check-list' of factors that appear to point to employment status, balanced against factors that appear to point to self-employed status. This was thought to be the most appropriate test, in that it amalgamates the control, integration and economic reality tests, recognising that although each points to an important factor, no one factor is determinative. In the case of *Hall (HM Inspector of Taxes)* v. *Lorimer* the court warned against the use of a single factor to determine the status of the worker. The court stated that all the factors should be taken into account and a picture painted from the accumulation of the detail. One should then stand back to consider the overall effect by looking at the detailed picture and taking a view. Not all the factors will be given equal weight or importance in any given situation. Every situation must be considered on its own facts.

This multiple test is the test currently favoured by Her Majesty's Revenue and Customs (HMRC), although, as we will see, the courts have moved on from this line of cases to impose a further refinement to this test. It is, however, a rather vague test that can result in unpredictable judgments. At a practical level, it is difficult for the employer to apply in order to be able to determine conclusively whether he is engaging an employee or a sub-contractor. The following cases are examples of the difficulties that the courts have had with the multiple test. It is appropriate to recognise that policy considerations have often had a large part to play in the outcome of a case – issues such as whether a worker should be able to rely on another's insurance policy. Such factors are particularly difficult for employers to be able to anticipate.[3]

Policy decisions have been seen to influence the determination of status in many cases. The case of *Lane* v. *Shire Roofing Co. (Oxford) Ltd* is a good example, which again serves to highlight the problem of distinguishing status where the parties themselves had been happy to consider the worker's engagement as self-employment for fiscal reasons. Mr Lane was a roofer who had traded as a one-man firm previously, but when work had dried up he started to work for others. When 'engaged' by the defendant roofing contractor on a 'payment by job' basis, Mr Lane fell off a ladder and suffered serious brain damage. He brought a personal injury claim against the defendant roofing contractor in order to benefit from its employers' liability insurance. To succeed, he had to show that he was an employee; as a self-employed contractor he would not have been covered by the policy. Much as the result appeared surprising on its facts, the court found him to be an employee and his claim was able to proceed. Two policy issues arise from the case:

1. Would the decision have been the same if the claim had arisen in the context of employment rights such as unfair dismissal rather than in such a severe personal injury claim? It appears that the court in this case may have been swayed in reaching its finding so as to ensure that Mr Lane and his dependants had some recourse and compensation for his injury.

2. What would the likely reaction be of HMRC in relation to this new-found employment status as regards non-payment of Class 1 National Insurance Contributions and employment income tax through Pay as You Earn (PAYE)?

In the course of the judgment in the *Lane* case, the court[4] emphasised the need to take a broad view of the status of workers in order to ensure that proper insurance arrangements are in place.

The overall employment background is very different today ... First, for a variety of reasons there are more self-employed and fewer in employment. There is a greater flexibility in employment, with more temporary and shared employment. Second, there are perceived advantages for both workmen and employers in the relationship between them being that of independent contractor. From the workman's point of view, being self-employed brings him into a more benevolent and less prompt taxation regime. From the employer's point of view, the protection of the employees' rights contained in the employment protection legislation of the 1970s brought certain perceived disincentives to the employer to take on full-time, long-term employees ... But, as I have already said, there were, and are, good policy reasons in the safety at work field to ensure that the law properly categorises between employees and independent contractors.

In *Transmontana Coach Distributors Limited* v. *Walker* the company advertised for a self-employed mechanic. Mr Walker applied. He was a motor engineer and had always been self-employed. Initially he was engaged on a part-time basis and two months later this was changed to full time. He invoiced the company weekly. His invoices were headed 'T Walker and Co.' This relationship carried on for seven years, during which time Mr Walker was responsible for making payments to the then Inland Revenue, the company's accountants being satisfied that Mr Walker was self-employed. The court held, however, that Mr Walker was an employee. The case is particularly relevant as it shows that neither the status of any worker for tax purposes nor the fact that he rendered invoices will necessarily be conclusive of whether he is an employee or a contractor for employment rights purposes.

In *Specialised Eyes (Optical Services) Limited*, the company traded as optical retailers through a nationwide chain of shops, engaging a large number of self-employed opticians to carry out eye examinations. Most of them worked only for the company. They provided eye tests and took a fixed fee for each test. The opticians were held not to be employees. The company's degree of control was limited to deciding in which branch and on which day the optician would be given the opportunity to carry out sight tests. The court found that the opticians where not 'part and parcel' of the company's organisation. They were contractors.

In *Filcom Limited* v. *Ross* the company carried out telecommunications contract work for clients such as BT. In a written agreement, Mr Ross agreed to provide services to the company. In the contract, Mr Ross was described as a 'Contract Staff Member'. Mr Ross held a 714 certificate, as issued under the old Construction Industry Scheme. His employment status became relevant when his contract was terminated for sub-standard work. Mr Ross claimed that the company had made unlawful deductions from his pay and the employment tribunal had to determine as a preliminary issue whether he was an employee. Despite the presence of the 714 certificate, the tribunal noted that Mr Ross had been given specific tasks to do. He was responsible to a site agent. Quality checks were carried out on his work. His pay was negotiated according to a set scale. Although the 714 certificate was a factor pointing to self-employment, this was not the only consideration. They decided that most of the contractual provisions pointed towards employee status.

The intentions of the parties and the label given to a worker regarding his status are also indicative but not conclusive. The courts have often found it difficult to reconcile the intention of the parties and the label given to a worker with the policy considerations that underlie their decisions. Courts usually have limited regard to intentions and labels and will look behind any label where they feel that the label masks the reality of the situation.[5]

It is clear from the evolution of the various tests that certain factors are of considerable importance in establishing status. Some of the factors that have been considered relevant by the courts in the various cases are set out in Table 2.1.

2.2.5. 'Irreducible minima' and the multiple test

The case law on this area has developed more recently, whereby the law has added a further nuance to the multiple test. In essence, case law has

Table 2.1. Indicators that the courts have identified of employee and self-employment status

Indicators of employee status	Indicators of self-employment
General duties	
The employee is likely to have a job description/title and to be under a duty to follow the employer's instructions.	Duties and responsibilities are likely to be much more specific and generally will be spelled out in the contract.
Control	
The employee will be under a greater degree of control from his or her employer.	Generally, he or she would be expected to rely on his or her own initiative in carrying out tasks.
Equipment	
The employer is more likely to provide the equipment, including major pieces. Provision of small tools/equipment is not unusual.	More likely to provide the means to carry out the tasks, including major pieces of equipment unless providing a labour skill only.
Time/place of work	
Regular/contractual hours more likely. Usually required to work on the employer's premises or as the employer directs. Likely also to be employed for longer periods (although short-term employment contracts are not necessarily inconsistent with employment status).	More likely to be able to choose hours of work. Not necessarily restricted as to workplace. However, contractual parameters for tasks/hours are not unusual. Less likely to have long-term contract (but long contracts not necessarily inconsistent).
Business/organisation	
Likely to be an integral part of the business.	The individual is likely not to be an integral part of the business. Likely to be in business on his or her own account.
Personal work	
The employee must carry out work personally and will usually be restricted from working for another employer. However, it is not inconsistent with employee status that an employee does work for more than one employer.	More likely to be free to provide an alternative worker to carry out the duties or to have assistance. More likely to have other sources of income. However, working for just one party is not necessarily inconsistent with contractor status.
Financial risk	
Little or no financial risk.	More likely to invest in management and provision of services. Often works on a fixed fee. More likely to risk loss and have the opportunity to profit.

Table 2.1. continued

PAYE/administration	
Will be salaried/paid a wage subject to employment income tax, payable through the PAYE system and to Class 1 National Insurance Contributions (NICs). The employee makes no direct charge for services.	Likely to charge a fee for services and pay own tax on trading income, Class 2 and 4 NICs and value added tax (VAT). Likely to run own administration. Likely to invoice for services.
Employee benefits	
Entitled to holiday and sick pay and to enjoy insurance arrangements through the employer. Potentially paid overtime. Subject to disciplinary procedures.	Likely to make personal arrangements for insurance to cover inability to work. Subject to termination and damages claims only under the terms of the contract.

determined that unless a relationship provides for two irreducible minima, there can be no employment contract. In other words, absent either one of these two minimum requirements, the individual will not be an employee or a worker. The two minimum requirements are:

1. mutuality of obligation, whereby the employer has an obligation to provide work and the worker has an obligation to undertake work when requested; and
2. an obligation on the worker to provider his services personally.

Mutuality of obligation

Whilst the courts have consistently talked about mutuality of obligation, the emphasis as to its absolute requirement to be part of the employment relationship has only recently been made clear.

The leading case of *O'Kelly* v. *Trust House Forte*[5] involved waiters who were 'regular casuals' in a hotel. One group of workers was given preference in respect of the availability of work over other casuals. Sometimes these workers worked longer hours than the recognised employees. They had no other regular employment and claimed they were employees of the company. However, there was no obligation on the hotel to provide work, nor were the casuals obliged to work when work was available. The court held that as there was no mutuality of obligation the casuals were not employees. The fact that the hotel gave preference to them did not amount to a legal obligation to offer them work, nor were the casuals obliged to accept the work. Interestingly, the parties' intentions were held to be important. The Court of Appeal noted that the custom and practice in the hotel and catering industry was that casual workers were not considered to be employees working under a contract of employment and held that the parties could not have intended that the casuals were to have employee status.

Casual workers represent an important category of workers. They usually work for short periods with breaks in between when no work is either offered or carried out. They can sometimes be seasonal. Casual workers usually also can choose without penalty whether to come to work or not. The employer only pays for the hours worked. Casual workers often find it difficult to achieve employee status because of the potential absence of 'mutuality of obligations'. Historically the courts have been reluctant to find that a casual worker was an employee. This has been reinforced by the House of Lords' decision in *Carmichael* v. *National Power plc*, where it was found[6] that casuals who worked as tour guides at a power station on an 'as required' basis were not employees. The House of Lords held that the casuals' case:

> founders on the rock of absence of mutuality, that is, when not working as guides, they were in no contractual relationship of any kind with the C.E.G.B.

The House of Lords confirmed that, to determine the employment status of the casuals, the following had to be considered:

- the language used in the letters of engagement;
- the way in which the relationship had been operated; and
- the evidence of the parties as to how the relationship had been understood.

As with the *O'Kelly* case, the parties' intentions were held to be important; it was accepted that both had intended for there to be a lack of mutuality of obligation and the House of Lords was not prepared to interfere with this intention. Interestingly, the House of Lords suggested that determination of the casuals' status could be undertaken solely on the basis of the letters of engagement if the parties '*intended them to constitute an exclusive memorial of their relationship*'.[7] Similar relationships may be established under a 'zero hours contract' where the work is intended by both parties to be undertaken by employees but where the pattern of work is intermittent. There may be a fine line between employee status and self-employed status in such cases and it is notable in the *Carmichael* case how the House of Lords and the Court of Appeal arrived at different conclusions on the same facts.

Recently, the issue of mutuality of obligation and its importance has been considered in three cases of note. The first case of *A.D. Bly Construction Limited* v. *Cochrane* considered whether mutuality of obligation was required in relation to the definition of a worker under Working Time Regulations. In the case, Mr Cochrane worked as a labourer for A.D.

Bly Construction in 2001. He was engaged on a self-employed basis and tax was deducted from his pay under the CIS. In December 2003 the parties entered into a contract (there had previously been no written contract) which contained, in summary, the following material terms:

- Mr Cochrane could send a substitute at his absolute discretion whom Bly could reject if the substitute did not have the necessary skills;
- Mr Cochrane was not entitled to holiday pay;
- Mr Cochrane was free to undertake other work at the same time as working for Bly;
- clause 23 stated that Bly 'is not obliged to offer contract or Works to the Sub-contractor [Mr Cochrane] nor is the Sub-contractor obliged to accept such contracts or Works if offered. The Sub-contractor is not obliged to make his service available. Specifically both parties accept that they do not wish to create or imply any mutuality of obligations whatsoever, at any time, either during or in between any individual contract for services.'

Mr Cochrane complained to the employment tribunal that he was entitled to holiday pay under the Working Time Regulations. The Employment Appeal Tribunal (EAT) dismissed Mr Cochane's claim and reversed the tribunal's decision. The EAT found that it was settled law that there must be mutuality of obligations in order for an individual to be a worker for the purposes of the Working Time Regulations. The finding of fact by the tribunal that clause 23 of the Contract reflected the true position and reflected the party's intention was fatal to his being classified as a worker.

The issue of mutuality was again considered by the courts in the case of *Cotswold Developments Construction Limited* v. *Williams*. It is important to note that in this case there was no express written contract between the parties and it would appear from the case that where there is no express provision, the tribunal is much more likely to find that there is sufficient mutuality of obligations. Mr Williams was engaged by Cotswold Developments in October 2002 as a carpenter on work that they were sub-contracted to do in relation to the London Underground. He had no written contract. He was dismissed in 2004. He presented a claim for unfair dismissal and non-payment of holiday pay. The tribunal found that Mr Williams had worked regularly for Cotswold for 21 months and there was no suggestion he had worked for anybody else. There were occasions when he refused work and others when there was no work available for him to do. He was paid a set amount per six-hour shift less 18% deduction under the CIS. He was subject to supervision and was provided with the use of a company van. Whilst the EAT upheld the appeal and remitted the case back to the employment tribunal, it made interesting findings on the issue of mutuality of obligation. Bearing in mind that there was no express contract dealing with the issue, the EAT made the point that an over-riding contract is not deprived of the requisite mutuality of obligation if the employee has the right to refuse work or where the employer may exercise a choice to withhold work. The focus must be on whether there is some obligation upon an individual to work and some obligation on the other party to provide or pay for it. The EAT held that where there was one contract as opposed to a succession of shorter assignments, it was a natural inference from the facts that the individual had agreed to undertake some minimum or at least reasonable amount of work for the employer in return for being given that work or pay.

The conclusion from this case is that where workers working in the construction industry are engaged over a period of time by a company, it is likely that a tribunal will find sufficient mutuality of obligation save where the express terms of the contract state otherwise and thus reflect the parties' intentions.

The relative ease with which the courts will infer mutuality of obligation where there is no express clause stating its absence was also made clear in the recent case of *James* v. *Greenwich Council*.

Personal service

As has been discussed, assuming that there is sufficient mutuality of obligation between the parties in an existent contract, the next issue the courts will need to consider when determining whether the person concerned is a worker or an employee, as opposed to self-employed, is whether the person performing the work is providing his services personally. As with the issue of mutuality of obligation, courts have held that it is an irreducible minimum that the individual provides his services personally for both classification as either a worker or an employee. In the *Express Echo Publications* v. *Tanton* case, the Court of Appeal made it clear that provision of personal services was one of the irreducible minima for a contract showing employment or worker status. Furthermore, in that case and in the case of *Staffordshire Sentinel Newspapers Limited* v. *Potter* an express clause in the contract providing for the right of substitution was held to show that the individual did not have to provide his services personally on the basis that the clause reflected the parties' intentions and could not be said to be a sham.

Again, in the case of *Real Time Civil Engineering Limited* v. *Callaghan*, it was held that the right of substitution expressly stated in the contract could only be disregarded if it is a 'sham', i.e. that it does not reflect the intentions of the parties. The case law reminds construction industry employers how helpful express provisions in contracts can be in determining status, so long as such clauses do reflect the parties' intentions. Conversely, the case of *North Wales Probation Area* v. *Mrs Edwards* shows the trouble that can be caused by a poorly drafted agreement. Intention is important. In the *Bly* case, there was an express right to substitute part of the individual's contract. However, the EAT did not interfere with the tribunal's finding and the EAT held that the tribunal had implicitly found that the qualified right to send a substitute under the contract did not remove the element of personal service; as the contractual clause did not truly reflect the agreement between the parties, viewed in the overall factual matrix.

The flow chart in Figure 2.1 sets out the courts' current thinking when determining status.

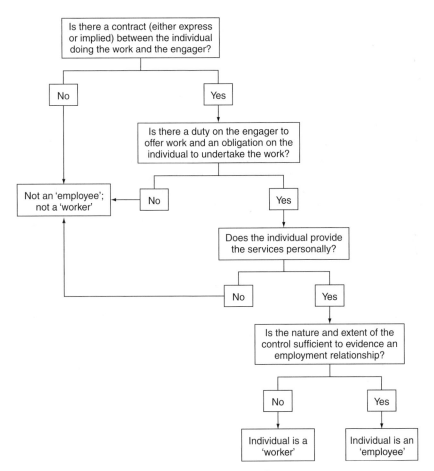

Figure 2.1. Employee, worker or self-employed

2.3. HMRC'S VIEW

A further complication arises from the fact that the status of the worker is relevant for a number of purposes and a different determination of the status of the worker may be reached for these different purposes. For example, the fact that HMRC has determined that a worker is self-employed for the purposes of tax collection does not necessarily mean that the worker cannot be an employee for the purposes of the employment protection rights.[8] It is interesting to compare the indicators that HMRC has stated it will take into account in determining the status of workers, which is produced in the accompanying box,[9] with the position taken by the courts. The list is in no particular order, nor is it exhaustive. No single factor or group of factors is conclusive. However it reflects those points upon which an HMRC Inspector will be focusing his or her attention.

Factors indicating employee status
- There is no risk of losing money in the job.
- Payment by the hour, day, week or month (especially unskilled workers) (HMRC places particular emphasis on this).
- No separate business organisation (e.g. yard, materials and workers).
- Works personally (no right to provide substitute, hire help or subcontract out duties).
- Supplies only small tools – 'traditional and normal in the industry'.
- Employer has the right to control where, when and what the worker does. The Inland Revenue places particular emphasis on the existence of a foreman/supervisor.
- Worker provides labour only and is more likely to be unskilled.
- Worker uses plant/equipment which the employer has hired (especially drivers, lorries, demolition plant, etc. HMRC places particular relevance on this).
- Longer period of work indicates employment status. The position may gradually move from a contractor status to an employee status.
- Regular work for the same firm of contractors.
- Employer has right to move the worker from job to job as priorities change.
- Moves from site to site with the same firm of contractors.
- Receives paid holidays/sick pay (especially long-term workers).
- Right to overtime.
- Contributions made to industry pension or sick pay scheme. Participation in schemes such as the Building and Civil Engineering Holiday Scheme.
- Union dues deducted from pay.
- Worker becomes 'part and parcel' of the employer's business.

Factors indicating contractor status
- Provides materials or plant for job, especially expensive or heavy equipment.
- Worker bids for the job.
- Takes risk of bid price being too low and risk of correcting faulty work at own cost.
- Fixed price work – same pay however long it takes. Worker may risk late completion. Analysis of basis of payment is therefore important.
- Can hire others to pay as substitutes. Can subcontract work.
- Worker works for a large number of companies/firms in a year.
- More likely to be a skilled worker.
- Concurrently provides same work for others.
- Renders invoices for work carried out.
- Has own place of business to take orders and store materials/equipment.
- Controls own hours of work to fulfil contractual obligations.
- Higher degree of expenditure on the job.
- Enters the day-to-day transactions of 'a true risk taking entrepreneur'.
- No overtime/sick pay/holiday pay.
- Paid by results (e.g. piece worker) – but this will not always denote contractor status.
- Registered for VAT (where relevant).

HMRC's considerations are clearly angled at determining whether the worker is 'in business on his own account'. HMRC's position as regards to the construction industry is specifically set out in their leaflet CIS349. This states that 'people cannot simply decide to treat working arrangements as either self-employment or employment. It is the circumstances of the working arrangement that determines how it is to be treated.' Whilst many of the factors referred to by HMRC are uncontroversial, there appears to be no reference made to the issue of mutuality of obligation in this leaflet (despite the guidance contained in HMRC's other leaflet entitled 'Employment status – employed or self-employed'. Additionally, CIS349 states that the right to substitute only 'suggests self-employment'. Accordingly, it would appear that the way in which HMRC puts the position in its leaflet CIS349 does not reflect the caselaw, which indicates that there are at least two irreducible minima required for employment status.

HMRC also suggests that the employment status indicator, which is its interactive tool, will assist a party in determining status.[10] Whilst

HMRC is to be applauded for seeking to try and provide certainty in this area, it is doubted whether the employment status indicator provides a true reflection as to status as applied by the courts, not least again as the irreducible minima that the courts rely upon do not appear to be reflected in the ESI.

2.4. SUMMARY

Clearly the lack of any single test to indicate employee status is unsatisfactory in practical terms, but in some ways the position is inevitable. The important point is that it is dangerous merely to make assumptions about a worker's status without actually reviewing the facts that lie behind the relationship. Additionally, the courts' focus on the irreducible mimima emphasises the important role which properly drafted contracts can play as an aid to classification. Whether HMRC will recognise this recent piece of jurisprudence will have to be seen. In some respects the distinction between employees and other categories of worker is being eroded by legislation, which uses different terminology when determining the type of worker who qualifies for the relevant statutory rights. For instance, under the Working Time Regulations 1998, a worker who provides 'personal work' qualifies for protection. A worker 'in business on his own account' is expressly excluded. Similarly, the definition used in the Minimum Wage legislation for the type of worker who will qualify for protection is

> an individual who has entered into or works under a contract of employment or any other contract ... whereby the individual undertakes to do or perform personally any work or services ...

There is a general trend in recent legislation towards expanding the scope of the workers to whom such protection applies, as the proportion of the workforce who are not employees grows. This may further increase if the government exercises its right to pass further legislation expanding the scope of statutory protection previously provided only to employees to the wider category of 'workers'.[11]

NOTES

1. *'Success at Work – Protecting Vunerable Workers, Supporting Good Employers'*, BERR, 30 March 2006, page 17
2. *Cassidy* v. *Minister of Health*
3. see further page 17
4. per Henry LJ
5. see *O'Kelly* v. *Trusthouse Forte plc*
6. overturning the Court of Appeal's majority decision
7. per Lord Irvine of Laing LC
8. see above *Transmontana Coach Distributors Ltd* v. *Walker*

9. see Inland Revenue leaflets IR56/N139, IR148/CA69 and 'Guidance on application of employment status rules to workers using intermediaries'
10. website address: www.hmrc.gov.uk/calcs/esi.htm
11. section 23 of Employment Relations Act 1999 which allows the Secretary of State to introduce regulations to make such changes

CHAPTER 3

Collective bargaining agreements in the industry

The terms and conditions of employment of a majority of employees employed in the construction industry are governed to a greater or lesser degree by a handful of industry-wide collective agreements. For example, it is estimated that between 500 000 and 600 000 operatives in the UK are employed on the terms of the Construction Industry Joint Council (CIJC) Collective Agreement. The scope of these various collective agreements correlate to the type of work involved. In some instances there is the potential for overlap between the collective agreements. This may be addressed directly. For example, the National Joint Council for the Engineering Construction Industry has reached an agreement with the National Joint Council for the Thermal Insulation Contracting Industry to cover situations where insulation or the removal of insulation is to be carried out on a major project and this forms an appendix to (*inter alia*) the National Agreement for the Engineering Construction Industry (NAECI) (see below). Where there is no such express provision, agreement will need to be reached locally as to which terms apply. It is important for employers to clearly define which, if any, collective agreement is deemed to apply to their employees. It will only regulate the terms of employment of a given employee if the employer and the employee have agreed to be governed by the terms of the agreement. Whether or not the employee is a member of one of the unions involved in the collective bargaining forum is immaterial. As such, the incorporation of a collective agreement into an employee's contract of employment is best provided by written agreement, for example, in a letter of engagement or a statement of particulars of employment.[1]

It may be that employers wish to offer contracts which incorporate some – but not all – of the terms of a particular collective bargain. There is no objection to this in principle; what is important is that an agreement exists between employer and employee with adequate certainty as to which terms apply.

Employers are obliged to provide their employees with details of any collective agreement which directly affects the terms and conditions of their employment, together with details of the persons by whom the collective agreement was made. As discussed in Chapter 1, this obligation is satisfied by the employer referring the employee to the collective agreement itself, so long as the employee has a reasonable opportunity of reading the collective agreement in the course of his employment.

In this chapter, five collective agreements are considered, namely:

- the Construction Industry Joint Council Working Rule Agreement;
- the National Agreement for the Engineering & Construction Industry (NAECI);
- the National Working Rules of the Joint Industry Board for the Electrical Contracting Industry;
- the National Agreement for the Heating, Ventilation, Air Conditioning, Piping and Domestic Engineering Industry; and
- the National Working Rules of the Joint Industry Board for Plumbing Mechanical Engineering Services in England and Wales.

The history and scope of each collective agreement is briefly considered. Some of the more important or unusual aspects of the respective collective agreements are also discussed and a comparison of their main terms is set out in the schedule on page 35.

3.1. CONSTRUCTION INDUSTRY JOINT COUNCIL WORKING RULE AGREEMENT

The Construction Industry Joint Council Working Rule Agreement (CIJC Working Rule Agreement or 'pink book') was established for the first time by the Construction Industry Joint Council (CIJC) in January 1998 through negotiations by the Building and Civil Engineering Joint Negotiators Committee following the demise of the Civil Engineering Construction Conciliation Board (CECCB). Prior to the CIJC Working Rule Agreement, terms and conditions for operatives within the civil engineering and building construction industry respectively were set by two separate bodies: the CECCB and the National Joint Council for the Building Industry (NJCBI).

The CECCB Working Rule Agreement dealt with operatives' terms involved in civil engineering work, whilst the NJCBI Working Rule Agreement dealt with the terms and conditions of operatives involved in building work in the construction industry. Basic rates of pay for crafts-men, skilled and general operatives were the same under both agreements. Amendments to both the CECCB and NJCBI Working Rule Agreements were negotiated by a body called the Building and Civil Engineering Joint Board (B&CEJB) which consisted of:

- Employers' representatives:
  - Building Employers' Confederation;[2] and
  - Federation of Civil Engineering Contractors (FCEC).
- Trade unions:
  - Union of Construction, Allied Trade and Technicians (UCATT);
  - Transport and General Workers' Union (TGWU – now merged into Unite); and
  - General Municipal and Boilermakers' Union (GMB).

On completion of negotiations, the B&CEJB would recommend that the two constituent bodies (CECCB and NJCBI) should ratify and pro-mulgate the agreement reached by the B&CEJB on basic rates of pay and allowances, into both working rule agreements. Amendments to the working rule agreements could only be made once the CECCB and NJCBI ratified the proposals.

In November 1996, the FCEC, one of the employer parties to the CECCB Working Rule Agreement, was dissolved by resolution of its council. In Octo-ber/November 1996, a leading barrister advised that, due to the withdrawal of the FCEC, the CECCB had effectively ceased to exist as the FCEC had provided representatives on the employers' side of the CECCB. This also meant that the existing CECCB Working Rule Agreement could not be altered or amended and that the CECCB ceased to have legal validity as an authoritative body over the CECCB Working Rule Agreement. It was recognised that some new negotiating machinery would need to be set up to provide collective agreements that reflected contemporary issues and rates of pay in the building and civil engineering industry.

As a result, the Building and Civil Engineering Joint Negotiators' Com-mittee was established. It had no constitutional or legal right to amend either of the existing working rule agreements, but it could make recom-mendations. It was this body that took charge of negotiations to establish a new authoritative body and a new working rule agreement.

Eventually, on 4 December 1997, the Building and Civil Engineering Joint Negotiators' Committee reached agreement in respect of an increase in the rate of pay of those operatives employed under the then existing CECCB and NJCBI Working Rule Agreements for the year 1997/1998. Whilst there was a question mark as to whether the CECCB and the NJCBI could ratify or promulgate this agreed increase in rate of pay, the increase was put forward to the CECCB and NJCBI member employers. Thereafter, on 1 January 1998, the CIJC was established, with a new national collective agreement (the CIJC Working Rule Agreement) being agreed to cover both the building and civil engineering sides of the construction industry with effect from 29 June 1998.

The 'Adherent Bodies' to the CIJC and the CIJC Working Rule Agreement are:

- Employers' representatives:
  - Construction Confederation;[3]
  - National Federation of Roofing Contractors; and
  - National Association of Shopfitters.
- Trade unions:
  - UCATT;
  - Unite – T&G section; and
  - GMB.

The aims and functions of the CIJC are stated at Rule 6 of the CIJC Constitution and Rules of Procedure to be as follows:

- To agree rates of wages and other emoluments of building and civil engineering operatives.
- To agree terms and conditions of employment for building and civil engineering operatives and to publish them as working rules for the building and civil engineering industry.
- To deal with disputes or differences involving or likely to involve any member or members of an adherent body to the Working Rule Agreement in accordance with the conciliation procedure.
- To consider proposals for, and to make amendments to, the Working Rules.
- At the request of either side of the Council, to consider any industrial or economic question which has or is likely to have a bearing on industrial relations in the building and civil engineering industry.
- To take all reasonably practicable steps to ensure that operatives are employed under the Working Rule Agreement of the Council.

Unlike the National Agreement for the Engineering Construction Industry, the scope of the CIJC Working Rule Agreement is rather ambiguous. The agreement does not make it clear whether it affects 'employees' or 'workers' or 'sub-contractors'. Working Rule 1 refers to those 'operatives employed to carry out work in the Building and Civil Engineering Industry'. However, the guidance notes state that it is the intention of all the parties that 'operatives employed in the Building and Civil Engineering Industry are engaged under the terms and conditions of the CIJC Working Rule Agreement'.

Multi-year pay settlements are the norm, stability being created by three-year deals.

Whilst the CIJC Working Rule Agreement sets out minimum industry rates of standard pay, the payment of bonuses is left expressly for

CONSTRUCTION INDUSTRY JOINT COUNCIL
STATEMENT
OF PARTICULARS OF MAIN TERMS OF EMPLOYMENT – APPRENTICES

All the provisions of the Construction Industry Joint Council (CIJC) Working Rule Agreement (WRA) whether expressly referred to or not, form part of your terms and condition of employment, unless expressly excluded and should be read in conjunction with this statement. A copy of the CIJC Working Rule Agreement is available for inspection at . . . .

Date of issue of statement . . . . . . / . . . . . .200 . . . . .

1a. Name of employer . . . .

1b. Employer's address. . . . .

1c. Place of Work (if different from 1b above and/or variable). . . . .
   At any time during your apprenticeship you may be transferred from one job or site to another job or site subject to Working Rule 14.

2. Name of Apprentice. . . . . Trade . . . .
   The employer will use his best endeavours to provide appropriate practical experience relevant to your type of Apprenticeship.

3. You have/have not had employment, which, counts as continuous with your current employment. Accordingly, your period of continuous employment began on . . . . / . . . ./20 . . . .

4. Your remuneration is paid by weekly instalments in arrears.
   On the date of issue of this statement your rate of pay was £ . . . . per hour in accordance with Working Rule 1.5.2 (£ . . . . per 39 hour week)

5. Your hours are 39 hours per week in accordance with Working Rule 3; Monday to Thursday from . . . . . am to . . . . . pm. & Fridays from . . . . . am to . . . . . pm. Additionally you are required to attend appropriate courses at college or other place of learning and are required to attend during the hours designated in accordance with the appropriate course as designated by the employer.

6. **Where work is temporarily stopped or not provided by the Employer you may be temporarily laid off in accordance with Working Rule 17.4.**

7. Overtime, which must be authorised, is calculated on a daily basis. Apprentices aged under 18 shall not be permitted to work overtime at the employers premises or site in accordance with Working Rule 1.5:4. Apprentices aged 18 and over may not unreasonably refuse to work overtime when required. Overtime payments will be in accordance with Working Rule 4 and, where there has not been unauthorised absence in the relevant week, shall be calculated as follows: Monday to Friday – first four hours after completion of normal working hours for the day: time and a half; thereafter until starting time next morning: double time.
   Saturday – first four hours: time and a half; thereafter double time.
   Sunday – double time until starting time on Monday.

8. Annual holidays – you are entitled to 21 days holiday per year – 7 working days must be taken in conjunction with Christmas Day, Boxing Day and New Years Day and 4 working days must be taken immediately following Easter Monday; the remaining 10 days are to be taken by mutual agreement with your employer between 1 May and 31 October each year – in accordance with Working Rule 18. Payment for all annual holiday shall be in accordance with Working Rule 18. If your employment commences or is terminated part way through the holiday year, entitlement to annual holidays and/or holiday pay will be in accordance with Working Rule 18. Public Holidays – You are entitled to 8 days public holiday per year. Entitlement to, and payment for, public holidays shall be in accordance with Working Rule 19. The Holiday year runs from the second Monday in January each year.

9. Absence and Sick Pay – The employer must be notified at the earliest practical time during the first day of any absence and no later than midday. The first 7 days may be covered by self certification. Thereafter absence must be covered by a certificate or certificates given by a registered medical practitioner. The apprentice shall be entitled to Statutory Sick Pay (SSP) plus Industry sick pay in accordance with WR.20 save the aggregate amount of SSP plus Industry sick pay shall not exceed a normal weeks pay in accordance with WR.1.5.2.

10. Pension and Benefits Scheme – You are entitled to payments in accordance with the Building and Civil Engineering Benefits Scheme Trustee Limited. Details of which are available from .... or from B&CE Benefits Scheme Trustee Limited, Manor Royal, Crawley, West Sussex RH10 2QP.

11. Length of Notice of Termination to be given:
By Employer:
In accordance with the Employment Rights Act 1996 Section 86 – (1)
By the Apprentice:
1 Week

12. This contract is for a fixed term, the date of completion will be:
day .... / month .... / year 20.........
This contract may be terminated at an earlier date in accordance with clause 11 above. The period of training may, by mutual agreement, be extended by up to one year.

13. Any changes to the terms of employment will be notified to you within one month.

14. Apprentices must comply with the Company Safety Policy. Copies are available from..

15. I accept the above statement of particulars of terms of employment

Signed .... Date..........................
The Apprentice

Note

1. DISCIPLINARY RULES are laid down in Working Rule 23.

2. GRIEVANCES, DISPUTES AND DIFFERENCES
Steps for dealing with any grievances you may have arising from or relating the employment to which this statement relates are set out in Working Rule 22.

3. CONTRACTING OUT CERTIFICATE
Contracting out certificate arrangements do not apply to your contract of employment.

4. POST APPRENTICESHIP
Whilst every effort will be made to provide continued employment following completion of the period of **apprenticeship this will depend on available opportunities and prevailing business conditions.**

It is understood that the company may need to process certain data about me, that may be categorised under the Data Protection Act 1998, as sensitive data for monitoring, statistical, reference and administration purposes. I also understand that I may have access to this information held on me in personnel files and on a computerised system, by appointment with the Personnel Department.

Figure 3.1. Written statement of employment suggested by the Construction Industry Joint Council (reproduced with permission of the Construction Industry Joint Council)

agreement locally. To this extent, the CIJC Working Rule Agreement differs from other industry collective agreements.

In line with the CIJC's aim to settle disputes and differences, the CIJC Working Rule Agreement provides for a conciliation procedure in case of disputes. Furthermore, strikes, lock-outs or other industrial action are prohibited until such times as the parties to the dispute have sought resolution through the conciliation procedure.

An interesting development in relation to the CIJC Working Rule Agreement is the emergence of 'Template' from Building and Civil Engineering Annual Holidays and Benefit Schemes.[4] The Template scheme has come about as a direct result of the changes that were needed in the Building and Civil Engineering Group (B&CE) holiday pay scheme following the introduction of the Working Time Regulations 1998.

3.2. NATIONAL AGREEMENT FOR THE ENGINEERING CONSTRUCTION INDUSTRY

The National Agreement for the Engineering Construction Industry (NAECI or 'blue book') first came into force in November 1981 to exert discipline over the engineering construction industry, which in the 1960s and 1970s was characterised in the words of a National Economic Development Office report: 'on all major contracts being late and over-spent, and by the existence of a highly unstable industrial relations climate'. Industrial disputes were commonplace because the agreements that preceded the NAECI were imprecise and left too many significant terms and conditions of employment to be negotiated at site level.

By the second half of the 1970s, a consensus had built up within the industry that there was an urgent need for change. Negotiations began which concluded in the creation of the NAECI and the National Joint Council for the Engineering Construction Industry in 1981. The implementation of the NAECI has led to a significant reduction in industrial disputes and an improvement in industrial relations.

The NAECI is negotiated between:

- Employers' representatives:
  - Engineering Construction Industry Association;
  - Thermal Insulation Contractors' Association; and
  - Electrical Contractors' Association, Scotland.
- Trade unions:
  - Unite – Amicus section;
  - Unite – T&G section; and
  - GMB.

The NAECI has been the subject of a complete review and revision, resulting in the NAECI 2007–2010. It is stated to apply to all individuals employed on work within the scope of the NAECI by companies in membership of a signatory employer association.

The key objective of the NAECI is to supply a modern, robust and 'fit-for-purpose' national employment relations structure which:

- enables engineering construction industry employers and clients to remain globally competitive;
- provide attractive terms and conditions of employment and greater security;
- provide a basis for improved productivity, resourcing and employee relations.

The NAECI is characterised by: its detailed drafting; relatively high basic rates of pay; a strict control over the extent of local agreement over wages and bonus earnings or 'second-tier payments'; the restriction of excessive overtime working; and the encouragement of progressive shift arrangements. The NAECI's detailed drafting is indicative of its intention to limit the scope for local bargaining and therefore the potential for disputes.

A particular feature of the NAECI relates to major projects, which are identified so as to determine whether additional employment relations support is necessary, given that the National Joint Council (NJC) will have a concern in respect of projects that are of sufficient size and significance to the construction industry as a whole and will want to monitor their progress closely. On a 'categorised' project, on-site industrial relations are managed locally by both the contractors and the unions with regional-level NJC support.

In order to co-ordinate the industrial relations policies of the various contractors on a 'categorised project', the local parties will negotiate the terms of a supplementary agreement which covers all the items which the NAECI allows to be locally agreed at site level (within the strict parameters set by the NAECI). On completion of the negotiations the local agreement is referred to the NJC for final approval.

3.3. NATIONAL INDUSTRY RULES OF THE JOINT INDUSTRY BOARD FOR THE ELECTRICAL CONTRACTING INDUSTRY

The National Working Rules of the Joint Industry Board for the Electrical Contracting Industry (JIB Agreement) apply to employers and employees engaged in the electrical contracting industry in England, Wales and Northern Ireland. Electricians in Scotland have a separate agreement with the Scottish electrical contractors. The two agreements have been entirely separate in the past, but the principal items are now gradually being harmonised.

The JIB Agreement first came into being in 1968 following a series of strikes and lock-outs in the 1950s and early 1960s which had given electrical contracting a poor reputation. Industrial relations between the unions and the employers' association were poor. The old Industrial Agreement allowed a wide variety of 'plus payments' for abnormal conditions and these were used as devices to claim increases in pay at site level and were frequently used for political purposes to stop production and construction. The unions, the employers' association and their respective members feared that, unless the situation was brought under control, the industry would suffer permanent damage and lose its highly trained workforce. After a new executive was elected at the Amalgamated Engineering and Electrical Union (AEEU), the AEEU and the employers' association embarked on a policy of negotiating long-term agreements to avoid the annual wage confrontation, which had been the norm in the past. The new agreement, which was signed in 1968, bought out all the locally agreed site payments and has succeeded in bringing stability to the industry.

The 1968 JIB Agreement, as well as providing for annual wage increases, also provided for the setting up of the JIB to replace the existing national and area Joint Industrial Councils.

The JIB Agreement is negotiated between:

- Employers' representative:
  - Electrical Contractors' Association.
- Trade union:
  - Unite.

The objects of the JIB are as follows:

'to regulate the relations between employers and employees engaged in the Industry and to provide all kinds of benefits for persons concerned with the Industry in such ways as the Joint Industry Board may think fit, for the purpose of stimulating and furthering the improvement and progress of the Industry for the mutual advantage of the employers and employees engaged therein, and, in particular, for the purpose aforesaid and in the public interest, to regulate and control employment and productive capacity within the Industry and the level of skill and proficiency, wages and welfare benefits of persons concerned in the Industry.'

The aim of the JIB Agreement is akin to the NAECI: the parties to the JIB Agreement seek at all times to develop a common approach to all the problems which are encountered by the industry not only in their own interests but in the public interest.

Today, the JIB is governed by its National Board which consists of ten representatives from Amicus, ten representatives from the Electrical Contractors' Association and a Public Interest Member. It meets under its independent Chairman, currently Sir Michael Latham. Sir Michael Latham is required not only to chair meetings at the JIB but also to ensure that, in its discussions, the JIB maintains its high principles of mutual co-operation and that the public interest also is taken into account.

In addition, there is a system of Regional Boards. The country is divided into six regions. Each Regional Board has at least five employers' representatives and five union representatives. The Regional Boards are responsible for everything that occurs within their region and can decide all disputes affecting the employment of labour within the JIB Agreement (although only the JIB can decide wages and conditions of employment).

The JIB Agreement, like the NAECI, sets relatively high national wage rates and there is virtually no scope for negotiation at site level. Overtime is discouraged by the JIB Agreement. The JIB Agreement relies on a clearly defined grading structure: from technicians to labourers to electricians.

On major projects, the JIB has recognised the need to harmonise the earnings potential of craftsmen employed in various disciplines. The Major Projects Agreement for Mechanical and Electrical Services complements the collective agreement applying to mechanical and electrical workers. This covers electrical, heating, ventilating, mechanical engineering and plumbing work.

There are provisions in the Agreement for local productivity and incentive schemes. Electrical contractors and their employees frequently organise more informal bonus arrangements. These do not tend to cause problems on minor projects but would not be tolerated on major projects.

As with NAECI, the JIB Agreement uses the derogations allowed under the Working Time Regulations 1998 and extends the reference period over which the 48-hour working week maximum is to be measured from 17 to 52 weeks. It also supersedes the provisions for weekly, daily and rest breaks contained in the Working Time Regulations 1998. The JIB has also produced extended 'Codes of Good Practice' to govern certain aspects of the employment relationship including:

- recruitment;
- written statements of employment;
- disciplinary procedures; and
- representatives' duties.

The JIB Agreement provides for a JIB Combined Benefits Scheme, which is operated by the Electrical Contracting Industry Benefits Agency. Special provisions are also made for certain industries including:

- shipping;
- oil and gas – onshore;
- cable work;
- specified engineering construction sites;
- major projects (as discussed above);
- highway lighting.

STATEMENT
of Employment Particulars pursuant to the Employment Rights Act 1996 and the Employment Rights (Northern Ireland) Order 1996 (the Acts) for Electrical Operatives (including Apprentices) employed under JIB Terms & Conditions

1. Name of Employer . . . .

   Address . . . .

2. Name of Employee. . . . .

3. National Insurance Number . . . .

4. (i)   Date of commencement of employment . . . .

   (ii) Date on which continuous service began (if different from (i)) . . . .

   (iii) Date of this Statement . . . .

5. JIB Grade . . . .

6. Your Terms and Conditions are as negotiated under the Collective Agreement known as the JIB National Working Rules. If you are an Apprentice your Terms and Conditions are in accordance with the JIB Training Schemes. Your Employment is conditional upon you working to these Rules and Industrial Determinations that may be issued from time to time.

   (i)   Your current rate of pay is . . . .

   (ii) You are a shop employed/job employed**/locally engaged operative (please specify).

   (iii) Your Shop Address is . . . .

   (iv) Your normal working hours are . . . . per week.

   (v)   Pay period: weekly/monthly/other (please specify).

   (vi) Holiday entitlement: Annual . . . . days; Public . . . . days.

7. You are entitled to payment for incapacity for work due to sickness or injury. This is currently . . . .

   . . . .

8. Pension and Pension Schemes. You are entitled to:

   join the JIB Pensions Scheme if operated by your employer*;

   join a stakeholder pension scheme designated by your employer*; or

   make your own pension arrangements if you wish*.

   A contracting-out certificate is/is not* in force in respect of your employment. (See note 6 overleaf)

9. Notice of Termination of Employment. The following notice is required:

Period of Continuous Employment	Employer to Employee	Employee to Employer
Less than one month	one day	one day
One month but less than two years	one week	
Two years to twelve years	one week for each year of continuous employment	one week only
Twelve years or more	Twelve weeks	one week

10. To be completed only in respect of Apprentices or Electrical Operatives with fixed-term contracts of employment for more than 4 weeks:

    The date of termination of your period of Apprenticeship*/the Deed of Apprenticeship*/or fixed-term contract of employment* is. . . . .

    Apprentice completion under normal circumstances occurs upon attainment of the appropriate criteria.

11. Copy of the Disciplinary Rules can be found . . . .

If you have a grievance or are dissatisfied with any disciplinary decision this should be raised with . . . .

. . . .

You should also notify your Unite the Union (Amicus Section) Regional Officer if you are a Member. If, after exhausting the internal procedure, your dispute remains unresolved, you may raise the matter through the JIB Disciplinary and Grievance & Conciliation Procedures (see note 7 overleaf).

12. Copy of the JIB Handbook, Industrial Determination and other documentation relating to your Terms and Conditions is available for inspection . . . .

. . . .

I agree that the Terms and Conditions set out above (a copy of which I have received) and the Terms and Conditions contained in the documents referred to above (as varied from time to time) are the principal Terms and Conditions of my employment.

Dated . . . .   Signed . . . .

* Delete where not applicable
** Under National Working Rule 10.4 the place of recruitment is the Shop and by custom and practice all Job Employed Operatives are transferable from job to job.

Published by the
Joint Industry Board for the Electrical Contracting Industry,
Kingswood House, 47–51 Sidcup Hill, Sidcup, Kent, DA14 6HP.   © Copyright JIB 558

Figure 3.2.   Written statement of employment suggested by the Joint Industry Board for the Electrical Industry, revised Dec 2007 (reproduced with permission of the Joint Industry Board for the Electrical Contracting Industry) ©Copyright JIB 558

3.4.   NATIONAL AGREEMENT AS TO WORKING RULES FOR OPERATIVES IN THE HEATING, VENTILATING, AIR CONDITIONING, PIPING AND DOMESTIC ENGINEERING INDUSTRY

The National Agreement as to Working Rules for Operatives in the Heating, Ventilating, Air Conditioning, Piping and Domestic Engineering Industry (HVAC Agreement) is negotiated between:

- Employers' representative:
  - Heating and Ventilating Contractors' Association (HVCA).
- Trade union:
  - Unite.

The HVAC Agreement was first issued in 1911 as a mechanism principally for establishing recognised pay rates for the trades then employed in the industry. The HVAC Agreement has developed and evolved over the years to set the basic terms and conditions of employment of operatives employed in the industry. The scope of the HVAC Agreement comprises work related to the heating, ventilating, air conditioning, piping and domestic engineering industry. This includes:

- all forms of piping, including gas installations and plastic pipework;
- all forms of boilers, including oil-fired installations;
- sprinkler (fire protection) installations;
- heated ceilings; ductwork erection; thermal insulation; and
- associated service and maintenance.

The HVAC Agreement includes a well-defined graded pay structure which reflects working practices within the industry and the integral part played by welding in much of the industry's activities. The grades[5] are defined by a combination of factors relating either to competence and/or conditions agreed between the two sides of industry and overseen through the National Joint Industrial Council (NJIC). The NJIC is also responsible for overseeing the industry's apprentice training arrangements.

Pay for annual and public holidays, sick pay and certain other welfare benefits (such as death benefit) is provided by Welplan, the industry's welfare and holiday scheme.

As with other Agreements in the industry, the HVAC Agreement reflects the view that it is in the long-term interests of both sides of the industry to have a directly employed labour force. The NJIC considers that employers should not employ sub-contractors who are not bona fide employers of labour observing the appropriate recognised wage rate and working conditions. The NJIC hopes that, by drafting this policy into the HVAC Agreement, the industry will underpin the directly employed labour force and prevent the industry's training effort being jeopardised by the use of self-employed operatives. The HVAC Agreement also uses the derogations set out in the Working Time Regulations 1998 to exclude the regulatory obligations in relation to weekly rest, daily rest and rest breaks, preferring to rely on the rest periods provided in the HVAC Agreement. The reference period for measuring the 48-hour maximum working week is also changed from 17 to 52 weeks.

As for bonuses and allowances, the HVAC, in certain circumstances, allows for:

- responsibility allowances;
- merit money (where payment is made at the option of the employer for mobility, loyalty, long service and the like, and for special skill over and above the norm); and
- target incentive schemes.

There is no industry-wide administrative apparatus for limiting or sanctioning overtime working but the HVAC Agreement recognises that overtime must be contained and provides that overtime should only be used in cases of emergency or urgency.

Table 3.1. Schedule of the main industry terms of employment

	Construction Industry Joint Council Working Rule Agreement	National Agreement for the Engineering Construction Industry	National Working Rules of the Joint Industry Board for the Electrical Industry	Heating, Ventilating etc. National Agreement	Joint Industry Board for Plumbing Mechanical Engineering Services
1. Date of Agreement	26 June 2006	6 June 2007	January 2007	14 February 2005	November 2005
2. Date of implementation of last wage increase	25 June 2007	4 June 2007	8 January 2007	3 October 2005	2 January 2006
3. Date of next wage review	30 June 2008	28 January 2008	To be arranged	To be arranged	1 January 2007
4. Rates of pay	Craft rate £9.72 Basic skill rate 4: £7.87 3: £8.35 2: £8.92 1: £9.27	Grade 6: £11.87 Grade 5: £11.35 Grade 4: £10.82 Grade 3: £9.23 – Adult £7.10: 16/17-year-old Grade 2: £6.26 – Adult £8.14: 16/17-year-old	All grades have varying hourly rates depending upon whether they are: • shop reporting; • job reporting (transport provided); or • job reporting (own transport) • London rates Technician: £12.61–£15.86 Approved electrician: £11.04–£14.09 Electrician: £10.06–£12.99	Foreman: £13.20 Senior craftsman: £10.90–£12.25 Craftsman: £10.00–£10.90 Installer/improver: £9.07 Assistant: £7.64 Adult trainee: £5.25	Operative: £9.94–£12.88 Apprentices: 4th yr NVQB: £9.62 4th yr NVQ2: £8.71 4th yr: £7.68 3rd yr NVQ2: £7.58 3rd yr: £6.24 2nd yr: £5.52 1st yr: £4.32

Table 3.1. Continued

	Construction Industry Joint Council Working Rule Agreement	National Agreement for the Engineering Construction Industry	National Working Rules of the Joint Industry Board for the Electrical Industry	Heating, Ventilating etc. National Agreement	Joint Industry Board for Plumbing Mechanical Engineering Services
	General operative £7.31	Grade 1: £7.10 – Adult £5.51: 16/17-year-old	Labourer: £7.78–£10.42	Mate over 18: £7.64 Junior mate 17–18: £4.91 Junior mate to 17: £3.55	Trainee 3rd: 6 months' emp – £8.68 2nd: 6 months' emp – £8.32 1st: 6 months' emp – £7.76
	Skilled operative additional rate no longer available	N/A	N/A However, responsibility money is paid between 10p and £1.00 per hour (as agreed locally) to supervisors	N/A Responsibility allowance: craftsman and senior craftsman: 45p–£1.35	N/A
5. Productivity bonus schemes and fixed rate bonus payments	As agreed locally	To be determined locally but shall not exceed £2.20 per hour worked	No rules in agreement Profit Related Pay allowed (subject to conditions)	Merit money can be agreed locally for mobility, loyalty, long service or special skill. Target incentive schemes are allowed – to be agreed locally	As agreed locally
6. Temporary lay-off	May be agreed as an alternative to redundancy Operatives expected to register as available for work at the local job centre after five days' inactivity	May be agreed as an alternative to redundancy	Conditional upon: 1. every reasonable effort to attend site; 2. employer shall make representations to the client to gain access; 3. AEEU shall be informed and shall make its best		

			to gain access; 4. operations should then be redeployed	May be mutually agreed in the event of industrial dislocation	Short-term alternative to redundancy
7. Guaranteed minimum payment per week	Payment for the first five days of temporary lay-off in any three-month period. Guarantee is lost in event of break in continuity of work due to industrial action on site, Tide work or work paid by shift	For employees employed for not less than four weeks, payment up to 38 hours at their basic rate for the whole or part of the pay week. Guarantee is lost if production on site is disrupted or industrial dispute has affected work and the employee has received one week's payment	Statutory guarantee payment. Payment for five days in any three-month period	For operatives with at least two weeks' service 38 hours in any normal week at basic rate Guarantee is lost if dislocation of production is caused by industrial action	Payment of $37\frac{1}{2}$ hours of hourly rate guaranteed for one week
8. Inclement weather provisions	Temporary lay-off provisions apply	Normal rate plus enhancements for those who have returned to temporary shelters. Otherwise, basic rate	Guaranteed minimum applies	Guaranteed minimum applies	Guaranteed minimum applies
9. Lodging/ subsistence allowance	£28.17 Where the operative is necessarily living away from the place he normally resides	Daily rate: £28.19 Weekly rate: £197.33 Special rates apply to public holiday, annual holiday, sickness and inner London	£28.35 per night	£28.10 per night	£28.35 per night

45

Table 3.1. Continued

	Construction Industry Joint Council Working Rule Agreement	National Agreement for the Engineering Construction Industry	National Working Rules of the Joint Industry Board for the Electrical Industry	Heating, Ventilating etc. National Agreement	Joint Industry Board for Plumbing Mechanical Engineering Services
10. Daily travel allowance	£3.35 to £11.85 (RPI linked) for travel between 15 and 75 kilometres measured one way from home to job/site. Fractions of kilometres to be rounded up	Two scales for distances over 2 miles to over 35 miles: Scale 1: for those employees who travel by their own means Scale 2: where suitable free transport is available Scale 1: £1.96 to £13.77 Scale 2: £1.29 to £9.23	Up to 15: Nil 16–20 miles: £3.01 + £4.11 21–25 miles: £3.99 + £5.20 26–35 miles: £5.26 + 6.35 36–55 miles: £8.38 + £8.38 56–75 miles: £10.26 + £10.26 Every 10 miles over 75 miles = £1.81 + £1.81	Scale 1 (within M25): 0–15 miles: £6.00 15–20 miles: £7.88–£8.19 20–30 miles: £11.64–£10.88 30–40 miles: £13.02–£14.12 40–50 miles: £16.69–£15.15 Scale 2 (outside M25): 15–20 miles: £2.19–£1.88 20–30 miles: £5.64–£4.88 30–40 miles: £8.12–£7.02 40–50 miles: £10.69–£9.15	20–30 miles = £1.45–£3.65 30–40 miles = £3.50–£8.50 40–50 miles = £8.65–£9.70 Payable in addition to fares Lodging allowance applicable to all journeys over 50 miles
11. Protective clothing. Tool payments, etc.	None provided	None provided	Safety helmets: locally agreed Protective clothing required by law: provided free of charge	Safety helmets and boots to be supplied. Operatives to supply rules and spirit level	Provision dependant on nature of job
12. Abnormal conditions	Stone cleaning: £0.61 per hour Tunnels: £0.16 per hour Sewer works: £0.26–£0.40 per hour	No rules in agreement	No rules in agreement	£2.99 per day	Graded Major Project Agreement
13. Height money (dependent on height work takes place)	45 m–90 m: £0.35 per hour 90 m (at 45 m intervals) extra £0.35	No rules in agreement	No rules in agreement	£2.99 per day	No rules in agreement*

	Col 1	Col 2	Col 3	Col 4	Col 5
14. Normal working week	39 hours Monday to Thursday: 8 hours per day Friday: 7 hours	38 hours Monday to Thursday: 8 hours per day Friday: 6 hours	$37\frac{1}{2}$ hours day workers $7\frac{1}{2}$ hours per day	38 hours	$37\frac{1}{2}$ hours/week $7\frac{1}{2}$ work hours
15. Shift and night working	All of the Agreements make provision for shift and night working, for which there are additional payments				
16. Entitlement to paid annual holidays in a full year	21 days (seven days winter; four days spring and ten days summer)	25 days (minimum of five at Christmas, five at another existing annual or public holiday and 15 by agreement)	As determined by the JIB Annual Holiday with Pay Scheme from time to time (currently seven days winter; four days spring and 11 days summer)	23 days (four spring holidays; 12 summer holidays; and seven winter holidays) Welplan scheme applies	22 days (ten days must be taken in the summer months)
17. Number of days of statutory holiday entitlement per annum	Eight days	Eight days	Eight days	Eight days	Eight days
18. Weekday overtime payment	Cannot be unreasonably refused @ $1\frac{1}{2}$ basic for the first four hours, then double time	National guaranteed rates: Overtime worked before or after normal working hours on weekdays shall be paid at Overtime Rate A Overtime worked after midnight shall be paid at Overtime Rate B until the task is complete Rate A: £7.70–£16.63 Rate B: £9.90–£21.38	Deprecated by JIB. However, Regional JIB may allow overtime in certain circumstances. Overtime payments only become due after 38 hours have been worked After 38 hours @ $1\frac{1}{2}$ basic 15% uplift for flexible workers, and overtime after 38 hours	Time worked over 38 hours per week @ Premium Rate 1 (up to £5.40 per hour)	'Strongly discouraged by the board' – hours in overtime not to exceed 48 hours Past 43 hours to be at $1\frac{1}{2}$ time. After 8.00 pm $2\times$ time

Table 3.1. Continued

	Construction Industry Joint Council Working Rule Agreement	National Agreement for the Engineering Construction Industry	National Working Rules of the Joint Industry Board for the Electrical Industry	Heating, Ventilating etc. National Agreement	Joint Industry Board for Plumbing Mechanical Engineering Services
19. Saturday overtime payment	Cannot be unreasonably refused @$1\frac{1}{2}$ basic for the first four hours, then double time	Overtime Rate A for the first four hours before noon, then Rate B	@ $1\frac{1}{2}$ basic until 3 pm, thereafter, double time or after six hours	Premium Rate 1 (up to £5.40 extra per hour) for first five hours. Thereafter, Premium Rate 2 (up to £10.79 extra per hour)	Double time after 1 pm
20. Sunday overtime payment	Double time	Overtime Rate B	Double time N.B. special call-out rates also apply	Premium Rate 2 (up to £10.79 extra per hour)	Double time
21. Sickness benefit (paid in addition to Statutory Sick Pay)	A maximum of ten weeks Industry sick pay (excluding the first three days)	A maximum of 26 weeks pay at £150 per week (excluding first seven days)	A maximum of 28 weeks pay at £150 per week	Up to 52 weeks. For first 28 weeks, from £4.90 per week to £179.13 per week For weeks 29 to 52, from £35.77 to £89.60 per week (depending upon the Credit Value Category for each grade)	Payable from 4th day of illness up to week 28 £14–£105 Week 29–82 £31.30–£75.25
22. Death and accidental injury	In accordance with the Building and Civil Engineering Benefits Scheme Death: £22 000	£20 000 permanent disability £20 000 death (any cause) £30 000 accidental death at work	JIB Insurance, Accidental Death, Dismemberment and Permanent and Total Disability Schemes: £15 000 permanent total disability benefit; £17 000 death benefits £67 000 death at work	Welplan scheme £33 600 death benefit; £17 000 accidental dismemberment; up to £17 000 permanent total disability benefit	Death = 2× gross earnings in full tax year prior to death Dismemberment/disability = £3500

23. Notice of termination of employment	By employee: Up to four weeks: one day After four weeks: one week By employer: First four weeks: one day Four weeks to two years: one week Two years to 12 years: one week for each full year 12 years or over: 12 weeks	By employee: After four weeks: one week By employer: Four weeks to two years: one week: After two years: two weeks; Two years to 12 years: one week for each full year of employment up to 12 years or over: 12 weeks Severance pay up to 103 weeks at between £3.66 and £5.96 per week	By employee: Up to four weeks: one day After four weeks: one week By employer: Up to four weeks: one day Four weeks to two years: one week Two weeks to 12 years: one week for each full year Over 12 years: 12 weeks	By operative: Up to five days: remainder of working day (more than two hours) Five days to four weeks: remainder of working week (more than one day) More than four weeks: one week By Employer: Up to five days: remainder of working day (more than two hours) Five days to four weeks: remainder of working week (more than one day) Four weeks to two years: one week Two years to 12 years: one week for each full year of employment up to 12 weeks	By employee: 1st week: two hours Up to four weeks: 1 day After four weeks: one week After two years: one week After 12 years: one week By employer: 1st week: two hours Up to four weeks: one day After four weeks: one week After two years: one week for each year After 12 years: 12 weeks
24. Pension arrangements within Collective Agreements	Building and Civil Engineering Easybuild scheme – minimum employer contribution £3.00 Where employee contributes £3.01–£10.00 employer will match up to £10.00	ECI Stakeholder Scheme £3.90 minimum employee contribution per week. £5.00 fixed employer contribution per week	JIB pensions scheme	H&V Pensions available – voluntary scheme	Employers must enrol employees with scheme provided by Plumbing Pensions (UK) Limited unless alternative scheme agreed

3.5. NATIONAL WORKING RULES OF THE JOINT INDUSTRY BOARD FOR PLUMBING MECHANICAL ENGINEERING SERVICES IN ENGLAND AND WALES

The National Working Rules are negotiated between:

- Employers' representative:
  - Association of Plumbing, Heating and Mechanical Services Contractors; and
  - Construction Confederation.
- Trade union:
  - Unite.

This agreement follows a conventional format. In terms of which operatives fall within the ambit of this agreement, there is clear potential for overlap with the HVCA collective agreement and the scope of the agreement is not well defined.

One feature of particular interest is the detailed procedure for conciliation, designed to resolve disputes between operatives and their employer. The mechanism envisages that most disputes will be resolved by the operative's supervisor or with the involvement of the shop steward. Where this does not happen, the dispute shall be referred by the Unite Regional Officer to a regional conciliation panel with appeal to a national level panel. A considerable amount of procedural detail may be found within the agreement.

Overtime is the subject of 'strong discouragement' and systematic overtime is only to be introduced to meet specific circumstances. The reference period in respect of the 48-hour working week is set at any 52-week period.

The Rules contain provision for bonus incentive schemes. These must be strictly related to targets and approved by the JIB.

The Agreement provides a sliding scale for the recovery of training costs where the operative leaves shortly after the employer has incurred the cost of the training.

NOTES

1. as the CIJC Agreement and Joint Industry Board (JIB) Agreements provide (see below)
2. as it was then called, now the Construction Confederation
3. formerly the Building Employers' Confederation
4. which is discussed in greater detail in Chapter 5
5. which were revised in August 1998

CHAPTER 4

PAYE/NIC – the clamp-down and the CIS

4.1. WHY EMPLOYMENT STATUS IS SO IMPORTANT

As a large number of employment-related rights apply only to a worker who is able to show that he is an 'employee',[1] the determination of a worker's status will have a substantial impact on the extent of the legal protection to which he is entitled. The employment status of a worker also impacts upon his tax position, determining the method by which HMRC will collect income tax and the class of National Insurance contributions (NICs) payable. An employee will have a payment on account of his employment income tax liability withheld at source by his employer through the PAYE scheme and will also have employees' Class 1 NICs deducted at source. His employer will be liable to pay employers' NICs. The self-employed sub-contractor, on the other hand, will pay Class 2 and possibly Class 4 NICs, depending on his profits, whilst his employer will pay no employers' NICs. The self-employed sub-contractor will have his income tax collected following the end of the tax year through the self-assessment scheme.[2]

4.2. EVOLUTION OF THE CIS

As early as the late 1960s, HMRC recognised that a number of workers who had been treated as self-employed sub-contractors in the construction industry were avoiding the payment of income tax and NICs. Whilst employees would pay employment income tax and Class 1 NICs at source through PAYE, significant numbers of workers claiming self-employment could not be relied upon to account properly for income tax and Class 2 or Class 4 NICs at the end of each tax year. In order to ensure that tax was collected from these sub-contractors on the 'lump', in 1972 HMRC introduced the Construction Industry Tax Deduction Scheme, with its accompanying 714 certificates and SC60 tax vouchers (the 714 Scheme). As such, any sub-contractor in the construction industry who attended site with a valid 714 certificate (which was issued by HMRC) could be paid gross of income tax. Otherwise, the sub-contractors would have lower rate income tax deducted at source through the SC60 voucher scheme. In both cases, the final tax assessment was calculated and accounted for at the end of the tax year by way of the sub-contractor's tax return. The system allowed HMRC to collect income tax at source from a large number of sub-contractors who had not been able to obtain a 714 certificate.

Over time, HMRC came to the view that the 714 Scheme was being abused. Whilst acknowledging that HMRC had itself 'turned a blind eye' to the abuse to some extent, it took the view that a large number of workers who were holding themselves out as sub-contractors (and who were working with 714 certificates or as SC60 voucher holders and being paid gross) would be more accurately categorised as employees. Frequently, HMRC discovered workers classified and paid as employees working on the same contracts, under the same terms of engagement, in the same way and on the same construction site as 714 or SC60 sub-contractors, whilst the two sets of workers were being taxed in different ways.

As a result, HMRC decided to review the taxation of construction workers in two significant ways:

- it introduced measures which sought to force construction companies to change the manner by which they classified their workers; and
- in 1999, it replaced the 714 Scheme with the Construction Industry Scheme (CIS).

These changes were designed to recover an extra £100 million in unpaid tax and NICs from the industry, and are commonly referred to as HMRC's 'clamp-down'. The CIS introduced more stringent conditions before a worker in the industry is entitled to be paid without deduction of tax. This allows HMRC to collect more tax at source with the worker having to claw back any overpayment at the end of the tax year.

4.3. THE NEW CIS

As of April 2007, new CIS legislation replaced the previous scheme.[3] Whilst the underlying principles of the old CIS remain in place, the mechanics as to how the CIS operates have been extensively revised with the new CIS designed to be simpler to use.

4.3.1. When does the CIS apply?

In order for the CIS to apply there needs to be:

- a payment;
- by a 'contractor';
- to a 'sub-contractor';
- in respect of 'construction operations'.

We will go on to look at these terms in more detail. Some carry a specific meaning under the CIS rules.

Payment

For the CIS to apply, there needs to be an actual payment of some kind (whether that takes the form of cash, cheque or credit).

As such, the CIS will not apply where an asset is transferred in return for the sub-contractor carrying out the construction work.

Contractor

The terms 'contractor' and 'sub-contractor' do not necessarily tie-in with the actual names of the parties. For instance, a person can be both a contractor and a sub-contractor under the CIS where there is a chain of sub-contracts.

There are two main types of contractor for CIS purposes. These are:

- actual contractors – i.e. a person carrying on a business which includes construction operations; and
- deemed contractors.

Anyone carrying on a business can be a deemed contractor if, broadly, his average annual expenditure on 'construction operations' in the three years up to the last accounting reference date has exceeded £1 m. If the business has not been in existence long enough for this test to apply, then that person can still be a contractor if he has incurred over £3 m of construction expenditure in the shorter period since the inception of his business. However, he can cease to be deemed as contractor if he can satisfy HMRC that there have subsequently been three successive years when expenditure on construction operations has been less than £1 m in each year.

Alternatively, various public bodies can also be deemed contractors if their average annual expenditure on construction operations over any consecutive three years (ending on 31 March) has been more than £1 m per annum. However, they too will cease being deemed contractors if there is any subsequent consecutive period of three years (ending on 31 March) in which expenditure in each year has been less than £1 m.

The public bodies to which this applies are:

- any public office or department of the Crown (including any Northern Ireland department and any part of the Scottish Administration);
- the Corporate Officer of the House of Lords, the Corporate Office of the House of Commons and the Scottish Parliamentary Corporate Body;
- any local authority;
- any development corporation or new town commission;
- the Commission for the New Towns;
- the Secretary of State if the contract is made by him under section 89 of the Housing Associations Act 1985;
- the Housing Corporation, a housing association, a housing trust, Scottish Homes or the Northern Ireland Housing Executive;
- any National Health Service (NHS) trust;
- any HSS trust; and
- any body or person established for the purpose of carrying out functions conferred on it by or under any enactment as may be designated as a body or person to which this section applies in regulations made by HMRC.

Sub-contractor

A sub-contractor is anyone who is party to a contract relating to construction operations where the contract either:

- imposes a duty on that person to:
  (a) carry out the construction operations;
  (b) furnish his own labour or the labour of others in carrying out the operations; or
  (c) to arrange for the labour of others to be furnished in carrying out the operations;
- or makes that person answerable to the contractor for the carrying out of the operations by others, whether under a contract or under other arrangements made or to be made by him.'

As such, the term is widely defined and includes the situation where a party in a chain sub-contracts all its obligations to other businesses.

The CIS does not apply to the relationship between a construction business and its own employees so, even if an employee were to technically come within the definition of sub-contractor, the CIS would not be applicable.

Construction operations

The term 'construction operations' takes on a wide meaning, going beyond just the construction of a building. It includes the following:

- construction, alteration, repair, extension, demolition or dismantling of buildings or structures (including offshore installations);
- construction, alteration, repair, extension or demolition of any works forming, or to form, part of land (including walls, roadworks, power-lines, electronic communications apparatus, aircraft runways, docks and harbours, railways, inland waterways, pipelines, reservoirs, water-mains, wells, sewers, industrial plant and installations for the purposes of land drainage, coast protection or defence);
- installation in any building or structure of systems of heating, lighting, air-conditioning, ventilation, power supply, drainage, sanitation, water supply or fire protection;
- internal cleaning of buildings and structures, so far as carried out in the course of their construction, alteration, repair, extension or restoration;
- painting or decorating the internal or external surfaces of any building or structure; and
- operations which form an integral part of, or are preparatory to, or are for rendering complete, all of the above operations (including site clearance, earth-moving, excavation, tunnelling and boring, laying of foundations, erection of scaffolding, site restoration, landscaping and the provision of roadways and other access works).

However, certain types of activities are specifically excluded from the term:

- drilling for, or extraction of, oil or natural gas;
- extraction (whether by underground or surface working) of minerals and tunnelling or boring, or construction of underground works, for this purpose;
- manufacture of building or engineering components or equipment, materials, plant or machinery, or delivery of any of these things to site;
- manufacture of components for systems of heating, lighting, air-conditioning, ventilation, power supply, drainage, sanitation, water supply or fire protection, or delivery of any of these things to site;
- the professional work of architects or surveyors, or of consultants in building, engineering, interior or exterior decoration or in the laying-out of landscape;
- the making, installation and repair of sculptures, murals and other works which are wholly artistic in nature;

- signwriting and erecting, installing and repairing signboards and advertisements;
- the installation of seating, blinds and shutters; and
- the installation of security systems, including burglar alarms, closed circuit television and public address systems.

4.3.2. What if the CIS does apply?

If CIS applies, then a number of different compliance requirements need to be met. Of these, the most significant is the question of whether the contractor needs to deduct tax from payments to the sub-contractor. Whether tax needs to be deducted depends on whether the sub-contractor is registered to receive payment gross or not. If the sub-contractor is registered to receive payment net, then the contractor will need to deduct tax at a rate of 20% (formerly 18%). However, where the sub-contractor is not registered with HMRC at all then the rate will be 30%.

In calculating the deduction, the contractor should first subtract the direct cost of materials. In order to be able to ascertain the direct cost of materials, the contractor is likely to need the sub-contractor to set this out. Where you are the contractor, consider including a contractual requirement on the sub-contractor to give you a statement setting out the direct cost of materials within a reasonable period before you are required to make a payment. Also consider including provisions enabling you to obtain evidence supporting any such statement and consider asking for an indemnity in the event of a false statement. You should also ensure relevant contractual provisions enable you to correct under-deductions by deducting a higher amount from future payments.

In most cases, the sub-contractor will be able to recover any VAT paid on acquiring the relevant materials. As such, HMRC's view is that the direct cost of materials should not include VAT unless the contractor is unable to recover that VAT. Again, relevant contractual provisions should reflect this.

In most cases, tax deducted by the contractor needs to be paid to HMRC on a monthly basis. This ties in with the normal PAYE month, running from the 6th to the 5th of the following month. The tax must be paid within 14 days of the end of each of these months (i.e. on or before the 19th) unless the tax is paid electronically, in which case the period is 17 days (i.e. on or before the 22nd).

Before actually making the payment, the contractor is required to check the status of the sub-contractor with HMRC.[4] This process is called verification. It is in this way that the contractor is able to ascertain whether the sub-contractor can be paid gross or net and, if they are to be paid net, the rate at which tax should be deducted.

Once the contractor has verified a sub-contractor then the contractor is unlikely to be required to verify the sub-contractor before making future payments under the same contract. This is because a contractor is only required to verify a sub-contractor if the sub-contractor has not been included in a contractor's return within the preceding two tax years.

In order to be able to verify any particular sub-contractor, a contractor will need to give HMRC not only the name of that sub-contractor but also the sub-contractor's unique taxpayer reference, accounts office reference and employer's reference. In addition, if the person is an individual then the contractor will need to provide his or her national insurance number. Where the person is a company, the contractor will need to provide its company registration number. Where the person is a partner in a firm, the contractor needs to give appropriate details both of the partner and of the firm itself. The contractor is not actually entitled to verify the sub-contractor until a contract is in place with that sub-contractor. As such, it is advisable, from a contractor's perspective, to include appropriate provisions requiring the sub-contractor to supply this information.

In addition to these requirements, a contractor also has to file a monthly return giving details of all sub-contractors paid in that month (running from the 6th to the 5th of the following month). The return needs to be filed within 14 days of the end of each month (i.e. on or before the 19th). The return must include a declaration by the person making the return that:

- none of the contracts to which the return relates is a contract of employment;
- he or she has verified all of the persons listed; and
- the return contains all the information, particulars and supporting information required to be included and that such information, particulars and supporting information are complete and accurate to the best of the contractor's knowledge and belief.

Even where a contractor has not made any payments in any particular month, the contractor is still required to file a nil return unless it has notified HMRC that it will not make any payments to which the CIS applies over the next six months.

4.3.3. Gross payment

If a sub-contractor is able to meet the business, turnover and compliance tests then that sub-contractor can apply to HMRC to be paid gross.

Business test

The sub-contractor must be able to supply specified evidence that it is carrying on a business in the UK which consists of, or includes, the carrying out of construction operations or the furnishing or arranging of the furnishing of labour in carrying out construction operations. The business must also be carried on to a substantial extent by means of a bank account. The evidence is as follows:

- the business address;
- invoices, contracts or purchase orders for construction work carried out by the applicant;
- details of payments for construction work;
- the books and accounts of the business; and
- details of the business bank account, including bank statements.

Turnover test

The sub-contractor must satisfy HMRC that its business is likely to give rise to a net turnover over the next 12 months which exceeds the relevant specified minimum. The relevant specified minimum for an individual sub-contactor is net construction turnover of £30 000 and the relevant specified minimum for a company is a net turnover of £200 000 or £30 000 for each director, or, if the company is close, £30 000 for each beneficial shareholder. For a partnership, the turnover test is passed if either:

- the business can show net construction turnover of £30 000 for each partner; or
- total partnership net construction turnover of £200 000.

In the case of an individual sub-contractor, the evidence required is effectively that the previous year's turnover exceeded the threshold. However, in the case of firms and companies that are only starting out, evidence of construction contracts under which payments will exceed £200 000 over the following year will be sufficient as long as evidence can be provided showing payments of at least £30 000 have been made already.

Companies that are wholly owned by companies which already have gross status under the CIS do not have to pass the turnover test.

Compliance test

The sub-contractor must have an excellent compliance record. This requires a high standard of tax compliance and compliance with company law filing requirements. Some failings are allowed but these are limited.

To pass the compliance test, a sub-contractor must, during the 12 months up to the date of the application, have done all of the following:

- completed and returned all tax returns sent to the sub-contractor;
- supplied any information to do with tax that HMRC may have requested; and
- paid by the due date:
  - all tax due from the business;

- ○ all NICs;
- ○ all PAYE tax and NICs due from the business as an employer; and
- ○ any deductions due from the business as a contractor in the construction industry.

Gross payment status can be cancelled by HMRC at any time if the sub-contractor fails to meet the conditions. HMRC can also cancel gross payment status if the sub-contractor fails to comply with his CIS obligations, whether in its capacity as sub-contractor or contractor (including a failing to file or filing an incorrect contractor's monthly return).

If HMRC refuse to allow or withdraw gross payment status, the affected sub-contractor can appeal the decision. The notice must state the sub-contractor's reasons for believing that the application should not have been refused or registration should not have been cancelled (as the case may be).

According to a letter sent out by HMRC to sub-contractors, HMRC has introduced a new annual compliance review process for construction companies to ensure that those that have been granted gross payment status continue to meet the qualification criteria. Companies will be selected at random by way of the CIS computer system, which will check compliance history, including PAYE, national insurance, self-assessment and corporation tax returns. Companies may not know that the review is taking place. Crucially, if it is found that, at the date of the review, compliance obligations have not been met during the previous 12 months, the contractor could lose gross payment status and be reclassified for net payment. Companies who find themselves in this situation will be able to appeal, before moving to net payment. A move to net payment could have a major impact on the company's financial and reputational status. It also puts great pressure on finance directors, tax directors, business managers and all related compliance services to ensure that the operational aspects of taxes management are dealt with accurately and on time.

What can you do to reduce the risk of losing 'gross payment' status?

HMRC acknowledges that some construction businesses experienced difficulties submitting their returns when the CIS scheme changed on 6 April 2007. Statistics released in September 2007 show that just 56% of companies have managed to submit their CIS returns and make payments to HMRC on time.

For this reason, HMRC has stated that in the first year of the new scheme arrangements, it will ignore all late submissions if they occurred in the first three months. Returns which were submitted late for the months ending 5 May, June and July 2007 will not be regarded as failures under the scheduled compliance review.

Going forward, HMRC has provided a margin of allowance for certain compliance errors, particularly when there is little or no impact. On this basis, the following will not compromise gross payment status:

- three late submissions of your CIS monthly return – up to 28 days late;
- three late payments of CIS/PAYE deductions – up to 14 days late;
- one late payment of self-assessment tax – up to 28 days late;
- any employer's end of year return (form P35) made late;
- any late payments of Corporation Tax – up to 28 days late, including where any shortfall in the payment has occurred an interest charge but no penalty;
- any self-assessment return made late; and
- any failures classed as 'minor or technical' in relation to obligations under the old CIS scheme where these fall within the 12-month period up to the application.

However, at the time of writing, HMRC stated that 19 October 2007 was the first date at which the legislation attached penalties to returns which had not been received. Despite a reportedly 'sympathetic view' being taken by HMRC, not least due to the postal strike at that time, some 86 000 penalties were issued to some 36 000 schemes. HMRC reported that four out of five contractors met their obligations.

4.3.4. Net payment

Where tax is deducted from payments to a sub-contractor, the tax is then set-off against other tax liabilities of the sub-contractor. Where the sub-contractor is not a company, the tax deducted is treated as income tax paid in respect of the profits of the sub-contractor's construction trade. If the sum is more than enough to discharge this liability then it is set against his liability to Class 4 National Insurance contributions.

If the sub-contractor is a company then the tax deducted is set against tax liabilities of the company in the following order:

- primary Class 1 National Insurance contributions in respect of earnings paid to its employee in that year;
- secondary Class 1 National Insurance contributions in respect of earnings paid to its employees in that year;
- income tax under PAYE in respect of that year;
- student loan repayments;
- refunds due to HMRC in respect of statutory sick pay, statutory maternity pay, statutory paternity pay or statutory adoption pay; and

- where the sub-contractor is also a contractor, tax withheld under the CIS in respect of payments made in its contractor capacity.

Where the sub-contractor is a company, any withholding tax remaining after deduction of all the liabilities listed above must be repaid to the company. However, this will only occur at the end of the tax year and only then if:

- the sub-contractor has filed all P14s and P35s; and
- there is no outstanding liability to corporation tax in respect of any accounting period ending before the date upon which the payment from which tax was withheld was actually made to the sub-contractor.

4.3.5. Employment status

In 1995, HMRC put the construction industry on notice that from 5 April 1996[5] the issuing of a 714 certificate by HMRC to a worker in the industry would not necessarily mean that that worker was a sub-contractor in HMRC's eyes. The 714 certificate could no longer be treated as conclusive of a sub-contractor's status. HMRC made it clear that the burden lay on employers in the industry to make sure that they had classified their workers correctly, whether they were 714 certificate or SC60 voucher holders. Employers were reminded that proper collection of income tax and NICs was down to them. Whilst this first stage of HMRC's clamp-down was recognised as introducing a fundamental change in the manner in which the industry engaged its workforce in that some workers were pushed towards employee status, there was no change in the law involved; the clamp-down merely introduced a change in HMRC's practice in enforcing the law.

To persuade the industry that this first stage of the clamp-down should be taken seriously, HMRC made it clear that it could seek from the employer repayment of all income tax for which the worker had failed to account in the event of deliberate avoidance or fraud by an employer. Alternatively, HMRC indicated that it would seek repayment of income tax back to at least the implementation date of the clamp-down[6] if an inspector found that an employer had incorrectly, albeit unintentionally, classified its workforce. Employers were faced with the possibility of substantial historic income tax and NIC liabilities as well as an increase in future labour overhead costs. Recognising that the new arrangements would have a significant impact on construction companies, both in terms of the potential increase in companies' labour costs and in terms of the difficulties in achieving an accurate classification,[7] HMRC and the then Contributions Agency issued leaflets[8] explaining to employers and to workers in the industry how, in HMRC's opinion, employment and sub-contractor status could be distinguished. These factors have been listed in Chapter 2.

4.4. CONSEQUENCES OF INCORRECT EMPLOYMENT STATUS AND FAILURE TO APPLY THE CIS

The changes made to the CIS and some comments made by HMRC in the run-up to the new CIS make it clear that employment status continues to be a major issue for those sub-contractors making significant use of labour-only sub-contractors.

As explained above, the CIS does not apply to remuneration paid by a contractor to its own employees. Employees should be paid under deduction of income tax under PAYE and National Insurance (and the contractors should account for employer's National Insurance also) – paying under the CIS is not an alternative.

Although HMRC has always made it clear that employees should not be paid under the CIS, it looks clear that HMRC is using the recent changes to the CIS as a platform for a renewed onslaught on this issue. In particular, by including the monthly status declaration, HMRC is seeking to direct the minds of contractors to employment status. The issue is important to HMRC because it can generally recover more tax in respect of employees (due to the employer's liability to employer's National Insurance contributions and due to more restricted expenses rules applying to employees) and because they receive the tax earlier.

For those contractors who are challenged by HMRC, the consequences could be very expensive for the following reasons:

- HMRC is likely to seek to recover from the contractors the tax that should have been deducted under PAYE together with associated National Insurance contributions.
- It also seems likely it will refuse to allow the contractors credit for income tax that has been deducted under the CIS in respect of payments to the relevant individuals.
- If the contractors cannot recover the income tax from the sub-contractors (particularly a concern if they have not put in place written contracts with each of their labour-only sub-contractors) then HMRC will treat it as a further benefit that the contractor has borne the individual's tax. As such, HMRC would expect the contractor to gross-up the tax liability – this would lead to an effective tax rate of 66% in respect of individuals subject to higher-rate tax.
- HMRC would demand interest.
- HMRC is likely to look for penalties – especially in the case of those contractors who have clearly not taken employment status seriously. Because the contractor will have signed a monthly status declaration, HMRC are unlikely to be sympathetic to such non-compliance.

Alternatively, some contractors may take the 'safer' option and treat all their labour-only sub-contractors as employees. Although this would meet with HMRC's approval, it would be likely to make those contractors less competitive. Not only would there be an additional tax burden but the additional statutory rights attaching to employees would also drive up the costs of those contractors.

Either way, there is a possibility employment status could have repercussions higher up the chain if it has the effect either of pushing up sub-contractor costs or of affecting the ability of sub-contractors to deliver on their contractual commitments.

4.5. CONSEQUENCES OF INCORRECT APPLICATION OF THE CIS

If a contractor does not operate the scheme correctly then there can be a financial cost. If a contractor does not account to HMRC for all tax that should have been deducted from payments to sub-contractors then HMRC can recover the relevant amount from the contractor.

There is also a penalty system in place for non-compliance:

- A penalty of £100 will be payable for each late monthly return. Where the return should have included details of more than 50 sub-contractors, there is an additional £100 payable for each additional 50 or fewer sub-contractors. Also, the penalty is due for each month that the return is outstanding.
- Where an incorrect monthly return is filed as a result of fraud or negligence of the contractor then the contractor is liable to a penalty up to 100% of the additional tax that would have been due.
- A penalty of up to £3000 may be charged if the contractor fails to:
  - produce records of payments under the CIS;
  - give sub-contractors statements of payments and deductions; or
  - fails to provide information or negligently or fraudulently provides incorrect information in the statements.

HMRC has indicated it will operate a 'light touch' approach to penalties at first. As such, it will not impose penalties for late filing of monthly returns (i.e. the penalties as referred to above) up to 30 September 2007. However, normal penalty rules will apply from 1 October 2007. HMRC has reported that some 86 000 individual penalties will be issued in November 2007.

However, a far greater threat to most contractors who are also sub-contractors will be the potential loss of gross payment status which could arise from non-compliance. Also, HMRC has made it clear that it will only apply the initial 'light touch' approach to the imposition of penalties – it will not extend to assessment of gross payment status.

4.6. EXEMPTIONS

The recent CIS changes also included some welcome new exemptions. The main ones are set out below.

PFI/PPP transactions

CIS will not apply to the contract payment between the public body and the main contractor provided that the following conditions are met:

- the person making the payment is one of the public bodies listed above;
- the payment is made under a private finance transaction – i.e.
  - (a) the resources are provided partly by one or more public bodies and partly by one or more private persons ('resources' takes on a wide meaning including funds, assets, professional skill, the grant of a concession or franchise and any other commercial resource);
  - (b) it is designed wholly or mainly for the purpose of assisting a public body to discharge a function or is ancillary to the function of a public body; and
  - (c) the public body makes payments by instalments at annual or more frequent intervals of fees determined in accordance with factors which include:
    - (i) the standard attained in the performance of services by the private person or persons in relation to the discharge of the function; or
    - (ii) the extent, rate or intensity of use of the resources or the asset which is constructed, enhanced, replaced or installed under the transaction.

However, the exemption does not apply further down the chain – it only applies to the contract between the public body and the main contractor.

Property used in own business

The CIS will no longer apply to payments made by deemed contractors who are not public bodies where the contract relates to property used for the purposes of the business of either that deemed contractor or a member of the deemed contractor's group.

Charities

The CIS will not apply to payments made by charities.

Reverse premiums

Payments which are taxed as reverse premiums (or which would be but for the fact they have affected the ability of the recipient to claim capital allowances) will not be within the CIS. Under the previous CIS rules, a landlord's contributions to a tenant's fit-out works would often be caught by the CIS. It seems likely this new exclusion has been introduced to ensure most such payments are outside the CIS.

4.7. PRACTICAL STEPS TO AID CLASSIFICATION

The greater the certainty which can be achieved by employers in determining their workers' status to HMRC's satisfaction, the better. In that respect, and in conjunction with the guidance set out in Chapter 2, the following steps might usefully be considered:

- **Keep records and notes of action taken**

  As HMRC has stated that it will not seek to recover backdated tax beyond the date of inspection where a 'bona fide' attempt at re-classification has been made, employers should be *seen* to have reacted properly to HMRC's policy. To evidence this, and in preparation for an inspection, employers should keep all records and notes of all meetings and advice received in relation to the issue. All papers should be kept in one place so that they are easily obtainable in the event of an inspection. File notes should record the decisions made and the basis of those decisions.

- **Reference to HMRC leaflets**

  Employers' decisions, in so far as it is possible, should refer to HMRC's explanatory leaflets.[9] These leaflets contain the particular factors which HMRC has confirmed it will take into account in judging the status of a worker. The more that an employer can be seen to have adhered to those factors, the easier it will be to persuade an Inspector that the employer's classification is correct.

- **Use of the employment status indicator (ESI)**

  The EIS is an interactive tool HMRC has developed that is intended by HMRC to help and advise contractors whether their workers are employed or self-employed. It is available at: www.hmrc.gov.uk/calcs/esi.htm. Whilst it is to be debated whether the ESI gives an accurate analysis of status as compared to current case law, if it is used, the ESI record should be retained.

- **Consider obtaining prior approval**

  Where an employer is unsure as to the status of a worker, or a group of workers, HMRC can be approached for a determination. Even though the approach may be made anonymously through the employer's solicitor or accountant, some companies nevertheless may be cautious about such action, due to the employer's fear that in explaining the background to the relevant workers' engagement, the employer's anonymity may be lost. It would also be reasonable to anticipate that HMRC would lean towards a finding of employment status in its determination.

- **Time/site records**

  Each employer should keep time/site records of:

- how its workforce has been engaged;
- the length of its workers' engagement;
- the terms under which they were engaged; and
- the manner in which they worked.

Without these records, it will be difficult for employers to satisfy an Inspector that they have properly classified their workers.

- **Draft sub-contractor/employee contracts**

  Employers should consider highlighting the differences between their employees and their sub-contractors in the drafting of their sub-contractor and employee contacts. In this way, the justification for an employer's classification can be made easier. These contracts should, where possible, include express reference to those factors which HMRC considers determinative as to status. These include terms dealing with:

  - an expression of a lack of mutual obligation;
  - the right to use a substitute or helper to do the job;
  - method of payment and invoicing;
  - tendering;
  - control;
  - financial risk;
  - right of dismissal;
  - part and parcel of the organisation;
  - length of engagement;
  - whether the work is piecemeal work;
  - whether the worker is entitled to sick and holiday pay;
  - supply of tools; and
  - declaration of intention of the parties.

  In addition, subcontracts should include:

  - the obligation on the sub-contractor to provide a statement of the direct cost of materials before the requirement on you to pay the sub-contractor (including VAT if applicable);
  - a right to demand evidence in support of the direct cost of material;
  - a right to be provided with the requisite information for the contractor to verify the sub-contractor;
  - a warranty that the employment status declaration and other CIS information is accurate; and
  - a right to deduct and vary the deduction of tax under the CIS if higher deductions are required in the future.

- **Changes in working practices**

  Generally, the issue of status is determined not only by a consideration of the contract terms but also by considering how the worker is engaged in practice. By showing a distinction between the treatment on site of sub-contractors and employees, an employer is more likely to be able to justify his classification.

NOTES

1. see the discussion in Chapter 2
2. subject always to HMRC's right to collect income tax at source under the CIS – see below
3. the new legislation is set out in sections 57–77 of the Finance Act 2004 and the Income Tax (Construction Industry Scheme) Regulations 2005 No. 2045
4. see Chapter 1 for discussion on employment status and next below
5. later put back to 5 April 1997
6. 6 April 1997
7. see Chapter 2
8. most notably IR148, IR56 and CA69
9. most notably CIS349 and 'Employment Status – Employed or Self-employed?'

CHAPTER 5

Working time

When faced with a tight deadline on a construction project, increasing the number of man-hours which are deployed on the project can be an effective way of accelerating progress. However, employers face a number of legal constraints which limit the extent to which the work-force can be required to increase their working hours:

- health and safety legislation on working time;
- contractual holiday entitlement;
- paternity and maternity rights;
- time off whilst sick;
- time off for family emergencies; and
- time off for certain extra curricular activities which have been considered to be for the greater good.

All of the above give workers in the industry the right to take time off work in certain circumstances, be it paid or unpaid. What is common to all workers of whatever status is that an employer must look beyond the worker's contractual rights and consider in addition the worker's statutory rights in order to see the full picture of the work-er's entitlement to time off work. This chapter concentrates on those aspects of these rights which give rise to particular issues in the industry namely the regulation of working time.

As discussed in Chapter 1, an employer is obliged to include a state-ment regarding an employee's hours of work and holiday entitlement in the employee's written statement of particulars. The collective agreements discussed in Chapter 3 set out the hours of work, minimum rest breaks and contractual holiday to which workers covered by those agreements are entitled. Whilst the relevant working rule agreements make use of the various derogations provided for in the Working Time Regulations 1998 (the Regulations),[1] the Regulations are nevertheless the source of a large proportion of the statutory rights which apply in addition to these contractual entitlements.

5.1. WORKING TIME REGULATIONS 1998

The Regulations came into force on 1 October 1998 and have caused significant problems in the industry. They were introduced by reason of the requirement to introduce into English law the provisions of two European Union directives,[2] both of which derive from European Union health and safety policy. As such, the Regulations must be interpreted purposively by courts and tribunals, to give effect to the health and safety objectives which underlie the directives.

The Regulations introduced new entitlements for 'workers' to:

- a maximum 48-hour working week;
- minimum rest breaks;
- paid annual leave; and
- special entitlements for night workers (including an entitlement to a health assessment and the transfer to day work in certain circumstances).

The Regulations were amended in 2003 to provide enhanced rights for young workers (above the minimum school leaving age but under 18).

5.2. SCOPE OF PROTECTION

The Regulations apply to 'workers' rather than just to 'employees'. Regulation 2(1) states that a 'worker' means:

an individual who has entered into or works under . . .

(a) a contract of employment; or

(b) any other contract

. . . whereby the individual undertakes to do or perform personally any work or services for another party to the contract whose status is not by virtue of the contract that of a client or customer of any profession or business undertaking carried on by the individual.

When applied in the construction industry, the status of so-called independent contractors is once again called into question.[*] The Department for Business, Enterprise and Regulatory Reform (BERR) (formerly the DTI) Guidance which accompanies the Regulations states that the term 'worker' will cover those individuals employed under a contract of employment as well as other individuals to whom an employer pays a regular salary or wage, provides the worker with work, controls when and how it is done, supplies tools and other equipment and pays tax and NICs. No guidance is given as to what is meant by 'performing personally any work'. The Guidance states that a worker will include agency workers and freelance workers but will not extend to self-employed people who are genuinely pursuing a business activity on their own account.

In the case of *Byrne Brothers (Formwork) Ltd* v. *Baird*, the EAT held that self-employed labourers who worked as sub-contractors in the building industry fell within the definition of a 'worker' even though their contracts provided that, in certain circumstances, the services they provided could be carried out by another individual. This right to send a substitute only applied if the workers were 'unable' to do the work and they also needed the company's prior consent.

In *Bacica* v. *Muir*, the EAT held that the fact a painter and decorator was required to perform personal service was not conclusive of his worker status. The EAT noted that many self-employed sole traders performed their services personally and may even secure business on the basis of selling their personal skills. However, if they provide those services as part of a business, they are not a worker but are instead genuinely self-employed. In this particular case, the fact that Mr Muir worked under the Construction Industry Scheme which entitled him to be taxed as a self-employed person, he prepared business accounts, he was free to work for others (and did in fact do so) and he was paid an overheads allowance and was not paid if he was not working, indicated that he was genuinely self-employed and that the services provided to Mr Bacica were part of his business activities.

Bacica demonstrates that there is a fine line between those self-employed labourers who qualify as workers (as in *Byrne Brothers*) and those who are regarded as genuinely self-employed. Although an individual's tax status is not decisive of his or her employment status, it was a significant factor in *Bacica* as was the fact that Mr Muir had other clients at the same time.

This raises the question of how an employer who hires an independent contractor can ensure that the independent contractor does not have 'worker' status under the Regulations. As referred to in Chapter 2, the answer may be for the employer to specify in the contract that the independent contractor is not required to work or to provide services personally. In such circumstances employers would be well advised to insert an express provision to that effect into their contracts, provided that such a provision would be consistent with the work which the independent contractor has been hired to do. This strategy appears to have been partially endorsed by the Court of Appeal in the case of *Express & Echo Publications Ltd* v. *Tanton*, a case concerning the definition of an employee. Despite the trend of previous decisions[3] which called for an analysis of what happens in practice rather than a reliance on the contract terms and the labels given by the parties, the Court of Appeal in *Express & Echo* held that if the contract contains a term that is incompatible with the relationship of employer and employee, the individual cannot be considered an employee. Whilst this case concerned the definition of an 'employee' as opposed to a 'worker', it provides a useful analysis of the importance of contract terms in defining the relationship and lends support to the suggestion that a provision whereby the independent contractor does not have to perform the services personally will ensure that he does not acquire the strategy of 'worker' for the purposes of the Regulations. Having said that, the courts and tribunals are bound to look to the purpose of the Regulations when deciding such questions. When there is any element of artificially attempting to place a given person into a given category, such manoeuvring must be treated with circumspection.

5.3. THE MAXIMUM 48-HOUR WEEK

Regulation 4(1) provides that a worker's average working week shall not exceed 48 hours. The High Court held in *Barber & Others* v. *RJB Mining (UK) Limited* that the right in Regulation 4(1) not to have to work in excess of a maximum of 48 hours on average in any week is a free-standing legal right, enforceable as an obligation of the employer under the worker's contract of employment or contract for services. As such, when several miners were instructed to work more than the maximum, the High Court issued a declaration that the miners were entitled to refuse to continue working in excess of the limit.

For young workers there are more stringent daily and weekly limits. They may not work more than eight hours in any one day and 40 hours in any one week (Monday to Sunday) respectively.[4] Whereas the working hours of adult workers are averaged over a reference period, as described below, there are no average provisions for young workers.

The average number of weekly working hours is calculated over a 17-week reference period and includes mandatory overtime hours (that is, overtime which a worker is contractually obliged to undertake). In some construction companies this can include half days on Saturdays. If a worker has fixed hours of work (i.e. 9.30 am to 5.00 pm), voluntary overtime is not included in calculating the number of weekly working hours where the employer has not required the worker to perform the work.[5] The Regulations permit the reference period to be extended to up to 52 weeks where there are objective technical reasons, or reasons concerning the organisation of work, which justify the extension and where there is an agreement between workers and their employers to that effect. As discussed in Chapter 3, the NAECI, the JIB Agreement, the HVAC

Agreement and the Plumbing Mechanical Engineering Services Agreement have all provided for the extension of the reference period to 52 weeks for workers engaged under the terms of those collective agreements.

Traditionally, the construction industry works longer hours in the summer than during the winter. It is therefore conceivable that during a 17-week reference period, falling within the summer, many workers would fall foul of the 48-hour rule whilst during a similar period in the winter their hours would fall within the 48-hour limit. Adopting a 52-week reference period would permit the excess and the shortfall to cancel one another out when calculating the average weekly hours over the longer reference period. The European Commission has proposed to allow member states to amend national regulations so that reference periods can be extended to 52 weeks without the need for a collective or workforce agreement. This was agreed in principal on 11 May 2005 but Members of the European Parliament (MEPs) demanded that additional safeguards were applied to ensure that the reference period was not extended without some form of initial consultation to protect health and safety. Matters have currently been put on hold pending resolution of the current issues over the future of the opt-out described below.

Many employers within the industry appear to be taking advantage of another way around the maximum working week, namely the derogation provided for in the Regulations which allows individual workers to opt out of the 48-hour limit. A worker may opt out of the maximum by signing a written agreement to that effect. Such an agreement (such as that show in Figure 5.1) may be terminated by the worker on not less than three months notice. Workers cannot be forced to opt out in this way but for so long as workers continue to be paid hourly rates, it is likely that many workers will be prepared to opt out to maximise their earnings.

The European Commission has expressed its concern relating to the increased use of the opt-out across Europe and recommended that, whilst it be retained, certain safeguards be introduced including: a limitation on its use only where a collective or workforce agreement cannot be used to negotiate agreement on working time; prohibition on the inclusion of opt-outs in the job offer or any probation period; maximum validity of one year and a maximum working week of 65 hours, unless collective or workforce agreements permit longer hours. However, as described above, on 11 May 2005 MEPs rejected these proposals and voted to abolish the opt-out within three years of a new directive being implemented. Several member states, including the UK, are intent on preserving the opt-out. They were consequently blocked by the UK in June 2005 of the Social Affairs Committee of the Council. At a further meeting of the Council of Ministers on 5–6 December 2007 it was agreed to postpone a decision on proposed changes of the directive and the opt-out. As such, its future currently remains uncertain.

THIS AGREEMENT is made the [   ] day of [   ] 200[ ]
BETWEEN

1.   [   ] ('the Company') whose registered office is situated at
      [   ].

2.   A N OTHER of [   ]

NOW IT IS HEREBY AGREED

1.   You hereby acknowledge that the Working Time Regulations 1998 (the 'Regulations')
      provide that a worker's working time, including overtime, shall not exceed an average
      of 48 hours for each seven-day period. Nevertheless, pursuant to the provisions of the
      Regulations, you hereby agree that such limit shall not apply in your case.

2.   Clause 1 of this Agreement shall remain in force indefinitely unless and until
      terminated by you by giving to the Company not less than three months' prior notice
      in writing.

3.   In order to comply with the Regulations the Company is required to monitor the
      amount of time you spend working. To enable it to comply with such a requirement,
      you agree to comply with the monitoring arrangements imposed by the Company
      from time to time including, where necessary, the completion of such records as the
      Company considers necessary for this purpose.

4.   You confirm that not withstanding the termination of the agreement evidenced in
      Clause 1 of this Agreement, you will comply with the monitoring arrangements with
      which the Company has to comply in accordance with the Regulations and to that
      extent Clause 3 above shall continue in full force and effect.

Signed by...
Signed by ....

For and on behalf of the Company
.... Name
.... Position
.... Date

Figure 5.1.   Example of a waiver agreement

Employers are obliged to keep, for at least two years, records of working time showing which workers have opted out.[6]

Following an amendment to Regulation 20[7] (dealing with unmeasured working time), employers need only concern themselves with recording their workers' pre-determined hours of work (if the hours are fixed by, for example, a provision in their contract) and those additional hours which the workers are *required* to perform by the employer. In such circumstances, employers need not keep records of workers' voluntary overtime. Despite this relaxation of the employer's duties, employers remain obliged[8] to take all reasonable steps in keeping with the need to protect the health and safety of workers to ensure that the 48 hour maximum limit is complied with.

5.4. HOLIDAY PAY, HOLIDAY ENTITLEMENT AND TIME OFF WORK

There are two aspects to holiday entitlements – the right to time off and the right to be paid during such time off notwithstanding that no work is undertaken. Such rights can be a matter of contract, to be agreed between the employer and the worker. Under the industry's various working rule agreements, workers are entitled to between 21 and 25 days holiday per year in addition to public holidays (21 in the CIJC Agreement and 25 in the NAECI). Traditionally, the industry has required part of this holiday entitlement to be taken over the Christmas and Easter shut-down periods and in the summer.

However, the Regulations once provide for a minimum entitlement for all workers who have been employed continuously for 13 weeks or more to four weeks paid annual leave. However following the BECTU case and a Working Time (Amendment) Regulations 2001, from 25 October 2001, this requirement has been removed.

5.4.1. Industry holidays and the regulations

It has been common practice for the majority of construction companies to provide for holiday pay through various schemes such as:

- the Building and Civil Engineering Industries Holiday Pay Scheme (now provided by B&CE Benefit Schemes through a benefits package known as 'Template');
- JIB Benefits Scheme; and
- Welplan

in recognition of the itinerant nature of a large proportion of their workforce. Under these schemes an employer buys credits for each operative who has worked for him, creating a fund so that when an operative takes a day's holiday he is paid holiday pay from the scheme. The purpose of the schemes is to ensure that each employer of the worker throughout the year contributes a fair amount to the worker's holiday pay entitlement. Whilst the schemes often provide other benefits (such as Death and Accident Benefits, and a range of pensions for workers) they merely provide for the payment of a cash sum and do not provide a right to take paid holiday. Historically, therefore, the amount of paid holiday workers were able to take depended entirely on their employers; the workers had no legal entitlement to demand holiday unless such a right was contained within their contract.

Furthermore, the value of holiday credits that were paid under some of the schemes was less than the value of a 'week's pay' that employers are obliged to pay under the Regulations (see below). Hence, the risk that participating employers would not be meeting their duties under the Regulations when they provided for holiday pay in this way. As a consequence, these schemes have been amended to ensure that participating employers are able to comply with the Regulations (see below).

Since the 1960s there has been in place an exemption from National Insurance contributions for such holiday pay schemes. However, the Chancellor's Pre-Budget Report 2007, delivered in early October 2007, announced the withdrawal of the exemption. Transitional measures apply in the construction industry.

5.4.2. Minimum leave

A week's leave is stated in the BERR Guidance which accompanies the Regulations to be the amount of time a worker works during a normal working week. So, for example, a worker who works five days a week is now entitled to 4.8 weeks annual leave. Until 1 October 2007, such a worker was entitled to four weeks' leave (20 working days) under the Regulations. A further increase to an entitlement to 5.6 weeks' leave comes into force on 1 April 2009. These changes reflect the government's intention to provide workers with 20 days of holiday plus eight days of bank holidays. It is to be noted that the taking of a bank holiday counts towards a workers holiday entitlement.

5.4.3. A 'week's pay'

The right to 4.8 weeks paid annual holiday is limited to the right to receive a 'week's pay' for each week of leave.[9] A 'week's pay' is the worker's weekly contractual remuneration where the worker has a 'normal working week', that is to say where a worker's contract provides for particular hours of work and where the worker works those hours. Where the worker does not have a normal working week, then a 'week's pay' will be the average weekly remuneration calculated by reference to the previous 17 weeks,[10] 26 weeks (in special cases[11]), or 52 weeks (if agreed). The remuneration to be included in the calculation will include any salary, wages and contractual overtime payments (overtime which the worker is obliged to work), commission or bonus payments received, but is unlikely to include travel allowance and subsistence payments. Once the total remuneration over the 17-, 26- or 52-week period has been calculated, the total number of hours worked over that 17-, 26- or 52-week period is ascertained. The average hourly rate can then be calculated from these two figures. A week's pay is the hourly rate multiplied by the average number of hours worked per week. Where a worker has worked non-contractual overtime, whilst the overtime hours are included in the calculation of the total number of hours worked, they are included at standard (not uplifted) hourly rate.

The calculation of a week's pay is as follows:

Week's pay = Average number of hours worked per week
multiplied by hourly rate;

Hourly rate = Salary *plus* bonus *plus* commission *plus* contractual overtime at higher rate *plus* non-contractual overtime at standard rate received over 17, 26 or 52 weeks

Divided by

Total number hours worked, including standard and overtime hours over 17, 26 or 52 weeks

Prior to its revision, problems arose under the Building & Civil Engineering Holiday Scheme (the 'Scheme') because the method of calculation of holiday pay under the Scheme was on an entirely different basis to that prescribed in the Regulations. Whereas the Scheme used basic salary only, the Regulations take into account contractual overtime, commission and bonus payments. The disparity between the two calculation methods meant that those workers who received holiday pay under the Scheme were unlikely to receive their full entitlement to holiday pay as provided for under the Regulations. To the extent that there was any shortfall in payment under the Scheme, employers had to ensure that they topped up those payments. The schemes have been amended to a hybrid, which allows payments to operatives for holidays from the contributions the employer has made. However, the obligation to provide holiday and as to the level of holiday pay each worker is entitled to is left firmly with the employer. In so far as the payments that a worker receives from the scheme are less than the worker's entitlement under the Regulations, the employer remains responsible to top up these.†

5.4.4. Employer's notices

It remains possible under the Regulations for employers to dictate to a degree when workers must take their annual leave entitlement.[12] Clearly this will be desirable in the construction industry where there are long established and traditional shutdown periods. Furthermore, it can also be used by an employer to avoid the need to make holiday payments at an inflated rate where a worker who does not have a normal working week proposes to take some holiday immediately following a 17-, 26- or 52-week period during which he has earned significant bonuses and commission payments. An employer can require his workers to take their holiday entitlement at specific times by giving them a notice specifying the days the worker is required to take. Workers must be given at least twice as many days notice as the number of days holiday. So, for example, where an employer wants a worker to take five days holiday, he must give the worker at least ten days' notice.‡

5.5. REST BREAKS

Construction companies are required to provide their workers with various minimum rest breaks.[13] The Regulations provide all workers with the right to a minimum daily rest period of 11 hours in each 24-hour period, a weekly rest period of 24 hours in each seven-day period (or 48 hours over a two-week period) and a rest period of at least 20 minutes where a worker is working for more than six hours a day.

Young workers are entitled to a daily rest of 12 hours, a weekly rest of 48 hours and shift breaks of 30 minutes in a shift of over $4\frac{1}{2}$ hours.

The entitlements to daily and weekly rest periods will not apply to shift workers when they change shift and cannot take a daily rest period between the end of one shift and the start of the next. There is, however, an obligation on the construction company to allow the workers to take an equivalent period of compensatory rest at an alternative time.[14] The NAECI, JIB Agreement and HVAC Agreement have all made use of the derogatives contained within the Regulations[15] to exclude the Regulatory rest breaks in favour of the rest breaks allowed for in each of the respective working rule agreements.

The impact of tight deadlines on construction projects may mean that it simply is not practicable to allow a particular worker to take his prescribed rest breaks. In circumstances where there is an exceptional and unforeseen surge of work, the Regulations provide that rest periods can be ignored, so long as the employer provides equivalent periods of rest as soon as is reasonably practicable. Alternatively, in exceptional cases, where it is not possible to do so, the employer must afford the worker 'such protection as may be appropriate to safeguard his health and safety'. The Regulations do not explain what is intended to fall within the definition of an exceptional and unforeseen surge of work, although it is submitted that as deadlines in construction projects are set in advance, there will be few circumstances when such time pressures qualify as an exceptional or unforeseen surge in work. It is likely that a heavy onus will rest with the employer to persuade a tribunal that rules laid down for the health and safety of the workers should be disapplied in a given set of circumstances.

5.6. NIGHT WORK

Where construction companies engage night workers, special provisions apply.[16] A night worker is defined as somebody who, as a normal course, works at least three hours of his daily working time during the night (the period between 23.00 and 06.00 or, by agreement, a period of not less than seven hours, which includes the period between midnight and 5 am). In the case of *R* v. *Attorney General for Northern Ireland ex parte Burns* a worker who worked at night one week in every three was held to work at night 'as a matter of course'. In the Attorney General's opinion, working at night meant no more than as a regular feature of employment. Whilst the majority of construction workers will not be night workers, site security guards and the like may well qualify.

Young workers cannot be employed during 10 pm and 6 am[17] or, where a worker is obliged under the contract to work after 10 pm, the period between 11 pm and 7 am.[18]

A night worker cannot be required to work on average more than eight hours in any 24-hour period. The reference period over which the average is taken is 17 weeks. Where, however, an employee's night work involves dealing with special hazards or heavy physical or mental strain, he must not work more than eight hours in *any* 24-hour period.

A night worker must also have the opportunity to undergo a health assessment before he commences night work and he must also be provided with the opportunity to attend health assessments at appropriate intervals throughout the period during which he is undertaking night work.[19]

5.7. ENFORCEMENT

Rights under the Regulations can be enforced in three ways:[20]

- by way of the Health and Safety Executive, which is the relevant enforcement agency with wide powers of investigation;
- individual workers can enforce the Regulations through employment tribunals. An employment tribunal which finds such a claim to be well founded may make a declaration to that effect and may make an award of compensation;
- following the *Barber* case (see above) workers may be able to bring claims for breach of contract in the High Court or in the County Court.

A worker has the right not to be subjected to any detriment and, in the case of 'employees' (but not mere 'workers'), a right not to be unfairly dismissed for seeking to exercise his rights under the Regulations. A dismissal on the grounds that an employee has:

- refused to comply with a requirement of the employer imposed in contravention of the Regulations;
- refused to forego a right under the Regulations;
- failed to sign a workforce agreement for the purposes of the Regulations;
- been a representative or a candidate for a representative of the members of the workforce in connection with a workforce agreement; or
- brought proceedings against the employer or alleged that the employer has infringed a right under Regulations

will be automatically unfair.[21]

NOTES

See Chapter 2 for further discussion on the issue of employment and worker status.

1. Regulation 23
2. the Working Time Directive (Council Directive 93/104/EC) and the Young Workers' Directive (Council Directive 93/33/EC). Following amendment, the Working Time Directive has now been consolidated as Directive 2003/88/EC

3. see further the analysis in Chapter 2
4. Regulation 5A
5. Working Time Regulations 1999
6. Regulation 9
7. as a result of the Working Time Regulations 1999
8. by the over-riding duty set out at Regulation 4(2)
9. Regulations 13 to 16 and sections 221 to 224 of the Employment Rights Act 1996
10. Regulation 4(3)
11. Regulation 21 (special cases include where the worker is engaged in security and surveillance activities or where the worker's activities involve the need for continuity of service or production)
12. Regulation 15
13. Regulations 10, 11 and 12
14. Regulation 24
15. Regulation 23
16. Regulation 6
17. Regulation 6A
18. Regulation 2(1)
19. Regulation 7
20. Regulation 28
21. Regulation 31 which amends section 45 of the Employment Rights Act 1996

* *R (on the application of the Broadcasting, Entertainment, Cinematographic & Theatre Union)* v. *Secretary of State for Trade and Industry* [2001] IRLR 559 SI 2001/3256.

† For an analysis of the lawfullness and appropriateness of 'rolled up holiday' see *Marshalls Clay Products Ltd* v. *Caulfield* [2004] ICR 436.

‡ For a view as to whether holiday pay should accrue for an employee who is, on long-term sickness, see *Kigass Acro Components Ltd* v. *Brown* [2002] ILR 697, [2002] IRLR 312, and *Ainsworth* v. *IRC* [2005] ILR 1149, [2005] IRLR 465, where on 16 December 2006 the House of Lords referred to the European Court of Justice.

CHAPTER 6

Guaranteed payment, minimum wage and deductions

The payment of workers within the construction industry is determined by agreement, either individually or collectively. However, regardless of what is agreed, a framework of legislation provides protection for workers:

- section 28 of the Employment Rights Act 1996 provides that in certain circumstances employees are entitled to guarantee payments;
- the National Minimum Wage Act 1998 provides for minimum hourly rates of pay for workers; and
- section 13 of the Employment Rights Act 1996 provides that employers can only deduct monies from a worker in certain circumstances.

6.1. GUARANTEE PAYMENT

A contract of employment in conventional format involves the employee reporting for work, doing a day's work and receiving a day's pay. However, where work is temporarily stopped or is not provided by the employer, the industry's working rule agreements allow employers to lay-off employees temporarily in certain circumstances.[1] In the Construction Industry Joint Council Working Rule Agreement, for example, operatives are entitled to set weekly rates of basic pay. These rates of pay are guaranteed, provided that the employee makes himself available for work, although the guarantee is lost in certain circumstances – for example, when the employer cannot provide work due to industrial action. The Joint Industry Board for the Electrical Contracting Industry provides that lay-off is not normally permissible, but acknowledges that there may be a strike on a site which has the impact of preventing the electricians working, notwithstanding that they are not in dispute and are available for work. In such circumstances they may be laid off and the statutory guarantee payments provisions will apply.

When an employee is laid off, rather than being made redundant, he has an entitlement as a matter of statute law to a minimum fall back payment known as a guarantee payment from his employer.[2] This entitles him to a payment calculated in accordance with the statutory formula for every workless day. The calculation of the statutory guarantee payment[3] is dependent upon the hours worked by the employee and his contract. However, it is to be noted that the maximum payment for any day is £20.40.[4] Furthermore, the number of days for which he can claim this payment is limited to an overall maximum of five days in any one period of three months. The right may be lost in some circumstances.

The purpose of the guarantee payment legislation is to compensate the employee for the loss, incurred through no fault of his own, of what he would have earned in normal circumstances. Payment is made for days which employees would normally be expected to work under their contracts of employment, but throughout which the employer has not provided them with work (because of, say, inclement weather or lack of materials). Some employees are excluded from this benefit such as:

- *Short-term employees*: i.e. employees employed under fixed-term contracts of three months or less.
- *Casual employees*: i.e. employees employed to perform a specific task which is not expected to take longer than three months.
- *Employees covered by collective contracting out*: i.e. where the Secretary of State has made an order[5] to exclude employees who are covered by a collective agreement which itself gives the employees a right to guarantee pay which is no less generous than the statutory right.

Such orders have been made in relation to a number of the industry's collective agreements. In 1977 the Working Rule Agreement to Civil Engineering and Construction Conciliation Board was ordered as an excluded collective agreement.[6] In 1996, the then Building Employers' Confederation and the National Federation of Roofing Contractors entered into an agreement with UCATT, TGWU and GMB, and obtained an order excluding those employees covered by the collective agreement.[7] The Electrical Contracting and Heating & Ventilating Contractors have not obtained a similar order in relation to these collective agreements and therefore only the statutory provisions apply.

- *Short service employees*: employees who have not been continuously employed for one month ending with the day before the workless day.

A 'workless day' is defined as a period of 24 hours midnight to midnight where the employee would ordinarily be required to work in accordance with his contract of employment, but is not provided with work by his employer by reason of a diminution of the requirements of the employer's business for work of the kind which the employee is employed to do, or any other occurrence affecting the normal working of the employer's business in relation to that kind of work.

As such, an employee cannot claim for a day when he would have been on holiday or off sick or where he has merely lost his voluntary overtime. Similarly, an employee has no right to a guarantee payment where the failure to provide work is in consequence of an industrial dispute.

An employee will lose his right to a guarantee payment on either of two grounds:

1. If he unreasonably refuses an offer of suitable alternative employment for the day.
2. If he does not comply with the reasonable requirements imposed by his employer with a view to ensuring that his services are available.

If an employee wishes to allege that he has not been paid all or part of a guarantee payment to which he is entitled, a complaint may be presented to an employment tribunal.

6.2.   THE NATIONAL MINIMUM WAGE

With effect from the 1 April 1999, all relevant 'workers' became entitled to the National Minimum Wage (NMW).[8]

6.2.1.   The rate of the National Minimum Wage

The rates are as follows:[9]

*   the main single hourly rate is £5.52;
*   for those workers aged 18 or over but less than 22, the rate is £4.60 per hour;
*   for those workers who are under 18 but no longer of compulsory school age, the rate is £3.40.

The genuine self-employed, genuine volunteers, apprentices under age 19 and apprentices over age 19 in the first two months of their apprentice-ships, are exempt from the NMW. Whilst the majority of workers in the construction industry are not immediately affected by the NMW, an understanding of the legislation is nevertheless necessary as:

*   the Low Pay Commission is obliged to review the level of the NMW; and

- there may be some workers who perhaps are paid a modest annual salary but who do such a large number of working hours that a construction company could be in breach of the NMW.

6.3. THE LOW PAY COMMISSION

The Low Pay Commission[10] has the central role in recommending the rate for the NMW and the basis upon which the rate should be calculated.

As with the Working Time Regulations 1998, the National Minimum Wage Act 1998 is applicable to all 'workers'. The definition includes any workers who undertake to do or perform personally any work or services.

6.4. CALCULATION OF THE HOURLY RATE

To ascertain whether an employer has breached the National Minimum Wage Regulations, the following needs to be considered:[11]

(1) The hourly rate paid to a worker in a pay reference period shall be determined by dividing the total calculated in accordance with paragraph (2) by the number of hours specified in paragraph (3).

(2) The total referred to in paragraph (1) shall be calculated by subtracting from the total of remuneration in the pay reference period determined under Regulation 30, the total of reductions determined under Regulations 31–37.

(3) The hours referred to in paragraph (1) are the total number of hours of time of work, salaried hours work, output work and unmeasured work worked by the worker in the pay reference period that have been ascertained in accordance with Regulations 20–29.

As can be seen, there are four distinct types of work identified for the purpose of calculating the total number of hours namely:

- 'time work';
- 'salaried hours work';
- 'output work';
- 'unmeasured work'.

Once the total number of hours in the pay reference period have been established and the amount of remuneration has been identified, an employer is able to calculate whether he has paid an amount equivalent to the NMW. In calculating the total remuneration, all monies received by an employee within the pay reference period should be counted. One exception to this is benefits in kind (other than those in relation to accommodation).

6.5. DUTY TO KEEP RECORDS

Whilst the National Minimum Wage Act 1998 does not require employers to provide a NMW statement to all workers, as was proposed when the legislation was being drafted, an employer has a general obligation to keep records which are 'sufficient to establish that he is remunerating the worker at a rate at least equal to the NMW'. These records must be kept for a period of at least three years. An employer in the industry should note the importance of keeping records as the onus of showing that a worker has been paid on or above the NMW is placed on the employer.[12] Additionally, workers have a right to require an employer to produce relevant records and to inspect the same.

6.6. ENFORCEMENT

In addition to a worker being able to bring proceedings in his own right in an employment tribunal or through the courts 'relevant officers who are appointed to ensure compliance' can bring proceedings on the worker's behalf. Currently, it is HM Revenue and Customs which is empowered to enforce the NMW.

6.7. DEDUCTION FROM WAGES

Section 13 of the Employment Rights Act 1996[13] provides protection to 'workers' from having deductions taken from their wages. An employer may not make a deduction from any wages for any worker employed by him or receive a payment from a worker unless:

1. it is required or authorised to be made by virtue of any statutory provision or any relevant provision of the worker's contract; or
2. the worker has given his prior written consent to the making of it.

Effectively, this prohibits deductions from a worker's wages (other than income tax and NICs or in compliance with a court order) unless the worker has expressly agreed in writing.

Matters are further complicated as a result of various cases that have taken a strict interpretation of the statutory exception that a deduction can be made where a worker has signified his consent in writing. Courts and tribunals have made it clear that not only must the consent be signed by the worker and be in writing but the consent must be drafted in sufficiently precise terms so that the worker knows precisely what amounts he may be allowing his employer to deduct from his wages and how that deduction is to be made.

A construction employer should therefore bear in mind section 13 particularly when granting workers loans or making payments for train-ing courses conditional upon the worker either completing the course or remaining employed with that employer for a period of time. The recoupment provisions in any such written agreement should be clear and unambiguous as to when, how and why the employer can seek to deduct monies from wages. Not only may the employer be required to repay sums wrongly deducted, but the right to recover may be lost in its entirety.

It is not to be forgotten that section 13 only relates to deductions from wages. Any freestanding loan agreement or other arrangement will be enforceable in the normal way by an employer as against his worker.

NOTES

1. see Working Rule 17.4 of CIJC Agreement, section 8 of NAECI, rule 5(d)(iv) of HVAC Agreement and Rule 7 of the 'Employment Practices' of the JIB Agreement. There are generally limitations on the employer's right to lay-off and wage guarantees may apply over and above the statutory provisions
2. pursuant to section 28 of the Employment Rights Act 1996
3. section 30 of the Employment Rights Act 1996
4. from 1 February 2008: SI 2007/3570
5. under section 35 of the Employment Rights Act 1996
6. SI 1987/156, now having effect as if made under section 35
7. SI 1996/2132
8. following the introduction of the National Minimum Wage Act 1998, which is supplemented by the National Minimum Wage Regulations 1999 (SI 1999/584)
9. with effect from 1 October 2007
10. established by section 8 of the National Minimum Wage Act 1998
11. Regulation 14
12. section 28 of the National Minimum Wage Act 1998
13. which consolidates the provisions of the Wages Act 1986

CHAPTER 7

Training

As the construction industry maintains its trend of continuing growth, the creation of an adequate supply of skilled labour is one of its greatest challenges. The industry employed 2.41 million people in 2005; forecasts suggest that more than 2.8 million will be employed by 2011, an increase of 17.5% over that period. With leavers taken into account, this means that an average of 87 600 new workers are required each year. This puts the issue of training into the spotlight.[1]

There has been much debate within the construction industry regarding the extent to which employers within the industry ought to take responsibility for training. Factors such as economic downturn and increased levels of sub-contracting had occasioned a period of serious decline in construction employers' involvement with apprenticeship training, with inevitable adverse consequences for the industry.

However, with the introduction of training incentives for employers, such as industry training grants, an increase in the requirement that operatives hold recognised qualification certificates such as those issued under the Construction Skills Certification Scheme (CSCS) and the demands of growing businesses, the importance of training has gained prominence in recent years.

Recognised training in the construction industry is provided mainly through the following channels:

1. Industry training organisations, such as the Construction Industry Training Board (CITB) and the Engineering Construction Industry Training Board (ECITB).

2. On-site training including apprenticeships, which combine on-the-job training and college study.

3. Higher education institutes and colleges of further education, including the National Construction College.

Prior to their abolition in 2001, there was a network of Training and Enterprise Councils in England and Wales which played a role in training within the construction industry. The Scottish equivalent, Local Enterprise Companies, still exist.

A network of Sector Skills Councils has been set up as part of the government's Skills for Business Network. These bodies are answerable to the government by reference to their performance against their Sector Skills Agreement. In the construction industry, the relevant body is Construction Skills. It is a partnership between the CITB and the Construction Industry Council (the representative forum for the professional bodies, research organisations and specialist business associations within the industry).

This chapter concentrates on the two statutory industry training organisations: the CITB and the ECITB. It should be noted that various non-statutory bodies exist, such as the Engineering Services Training Trust Limited,[2] J.T. Limited[3] and National Electrotechnical Training.

7.1. EMPLOYERS' OBLIGATIONS

There are certain sectors of the construction industry where operatives must have received some kind of recognised training or qualification before they are allowed on site. For example, gas installers must be registered (which means establishing that the applicant holds the appropriate qualifications) with CORGI (the Council for Registered Gas Installers) and have the relevant Accredited Certification Scheme (ACS) accreditation. Assessments are carried out with regard to the types of work undertaken and require periodic renewal.

Not all sectors of the construction industry are subject to exacting legal training requirements such as those which apply to gas installers. However, in many cases workers will be required to have attained a certain level of qualification as a result of their employer having entered into a contractual obligation to deploy skilled and qualified workers. Workers working on sensitive sites, such as petrochemical refinery plants, are required by contract to go through certain recognised checks. Most contractors and clients now require workers to be on an approved industry training programme and to carry cards to verify their skills before being allowed on site. This is particularly so in relation to basic health and safety training. Consequently various card schemes are available for the purposes of the various trades.

The CSCS was designed to meet this requirement and is the largest card scheme in the industry. More than 1 million cards have been issued since the scheme was set up in 1995. Various different card types are available depending on the level of skill of the potential card holder. A multitude of occupations are eligible for the CSCS cards (including painting and decorating, carpentry and joinery, and bricklaying).

7.2. THE ROLES OF THE CITB AND THE ECITB IN TRAINING
7.2.1. CITB
The CITB was established in 1964[4] in order to improve the quality of the training and the facilities available for training in the construction industry. It ensures that the quality of training is maintained at a high level by approving courses and by setting standards which must be met in order to obtain the appropriate qualifications. It also ensures that sufficient places are available on training courses to meet the industry's needs.

The CITB is involved primarily in the training of apprentices and young workers. It provides grants to employers who take on trainees and will assist young workers in securing a job.

The CITB oversees a number of training courses, such as Young Apprenticeships and the Construction Apprentice Scheme (CAS) and helps to provide funding for National Vocational Qualification/Scottish Vocational Qualification (NVQ/SVQ) courses and further/higher education courses.

The National Construction College is the training division of Construction Skills. It has five campuses around the country, providing a range of training courses dedicated to the requirements of the industry.

7.2.2. ECITB
The ECITB was established in July 1991[5] in recognition of the role which the engineering construction industry plays in the UK economy. The ECITB provides all aspects of training for the engineering sector of the construction industry, ranging from site skills to head office and management requirements. Its aim is to maintain a well trained workforce at all levels.

It organises a large number of initiatives including vocational qualifications and training programmes. In particular, it runs schemes approved by the National Joint Council for the Engineering Construction Industry leading to qualification as an engineer, namely:

- the National Skills Development Scheme which provides employees with a route to Craftsman and Advance Craftsman grades through training, assessment and experience; and
- the ECITB Apprenticeship Scheme for Engineering Construction for training in the trades of erector, mechanical fitter, pipe fitter, plater and welder.

It also runs the Supervisory Management Training and Development Scheme for management-level positions and project management short courses.

The Board, which is made up of clients, employers, trade unions and education specialists, also provides general support and advice to those in the industry, including research and careers information.

7.3. FUNDING

Both the CITB and the ECITB are entitled[6] to raise a levy from every company[7] engaged in the construction or engineering construction industry[8] in order to fund their work. Once a levy has been raised, it is recoverable as an ordinary debt owed to the CITB/ECITB, normally by way of a claim in the County Courts. Both the CITB and ECITB only provide training grants to those companies which are registered with the CITB and ECITB respectively (to assist the CITB and ECITB in their administration) and have paid their levy up to date. Small employers that are exempt from the levy may still qualify for grants.

7.3.1. CITB

The CITB's levy is based on the number of people working for an employer. Employers complete a return each spring (April) and the levy is based on the workforce and the wage bill. Those with a wage bill of £73 000 or more (including payments to labour-only sub-contractors) are liable. The contribution rates are set by Parliament annually.[9] The current rates payable by the employer are:

- 0.5% of payroll in respect of employees employed under contracts of service or apprenticeship; and
- 1.5% of net payments to labour-only sub-contractors.

The funding of the CITB has been hit hard by the HMRC clamp-down and the move from self-employed workers to employees, as independent sub-contractors pay a higher levy than companies which employ workers directly.

7.3.2. ECITB

The ECITB's levy is similarly based on the wages bill. The current rates are:

- 1.5% of the total emoluments (i.e. payments which are assessable to employment income tax) of all site employees and total net labour-only payments for site employees, where that sum exceeds £275 000 in the tax year; and
- 0.18% of the total emoluments of all off-site employees and the total net labour-only payments for off-site employees, where that sum exceeds £1 000 000.

Accordingly, for those employees whose on-site wages and off-site wages do not exceed £275 000 and £1 000 000 respectively in the tax year, they are exempt from the levy in view of their small number of employees.[10]

A Statutory Manpower Payment Return is sent to the employer every April which they must complete and return the ECITB giving details of total revenue, staffing levels and labour-only payments.

7.4. FUNDING CRITICISMS
7.4.1. CITB

The CITB's levy is particularly unpopular and is considered by many employers to be unfair. The main criticisms are that:

- large employers object to paying the training expenses of smaller employers;
- the paperwork to calculate the levy and to apply for training grants is complex and time consuming; and
- too much of the money going to the CITB is used up in administration rather than for actual training.

7.4.2. ECITB

The ECITB is subjected to less criticism as the levy is seen to be more fairly distributed and a greater proportion of the funds are used solely for training.

7.5. FUNDING SUGGESTIONS

It has been suggested that the levies should be on materials so that everyone in the industry makes some contribution to raising the standards through the means of training.

NOTES

1. source: Construction Skills Network: Blueprint for UK Construction Skills 2007-11
2. which has developed a modern apprenticeship model framework for the heating, ventilating, air conditioning, piping and domestic engineering sector
3. the industry-owned (jointly by the electrical contractors and Amicus) training provider in England and Wales for the electrical installation industry and allied industries
4. SI 1964/1079, and the Industrial Training Act 1982 (as amended by the Employment Act 1989 (s38))
5. SI 1964/1086, SI 1991/1305, SI 1999/158 and the Industrial Training Act 1982
6. in accordance with the Industrial Training Act 1982
7. see below for CITB and ECITB small employer exemptions
8. as defined in SI 1964/1079 and SI 1999/159, and SI 1964/1086, SI 1991/1305, SI 1999/158 and SI 2000/433
9. see draft statutory instrument which may increase threshold to £76 000
10. as allowed for under s11(3) of the Industrial Training Act 1982

CHAPTER 8

Immigration

Immigration law issues have assumed a greater significance for employees in the construction industry over recent years. To some extent, this can be attributed to changes in law and policy. A significant factor has been the shortage of skilled labour, potentially the greatest challenge facing the industry today. Even prior to winning the Olympic bid, observers estimated that the industry needed to recruit at least 88 000 people each year, with a wide range of skills, in order to keep up with growth in areas such as the house building sector. The dearth in home-grown apprentices and the expansion of the EU (and the consequent freedom of movement for workers from the former Eastern bloc) means employers are increasingly left with little choice but to employ migrant workers. According to research conducted by the Construction Confederation in 2004, there were around 100 000 migrant workers already employed on building sites throughout the UK. Figures released in 2005 showed that 130 000 individuals from eastern Europe had registered to work in the UK since their states joined the EU. These figures have continued to climb.

8.1. IMMIGRATION CHECKS

Frequent demands for immediate resources within the construction industry mean that it can sometimes be tempting to overlook the requirement to check the immigration status of individuals before they start work. Having to carry out immigration checks on every individual worker can be a cumbersome, time-consuming and unattractive task.

However, employers should be extremely wary of succumbing to such pressures by not fulfilling the statutory obligation to carry out immigration checks pursuant to section 8 of the Asylum and Immigration Act 1996 (the Act), because it is a criminal offence to employ someone, aged 16 or over, who has no right to work in the UK.

Failure to carry out the immigration checks required by the Act may result in the employer being found guilty of a criminal offence. This is punishable by a fine of up to £5000 for each person whom the employer is found to have employed illegally. Additionally, directors and officers could be found personally criminally liable for the offence and fined accordingly.

From 29 February 2008, the maximum civil penalty for employing someone illegally increased to £10 000 per illegal worker. It is also intended that a new criminal offence of knowingly employing an illegal migrant will be introduced for which it is intended that the penalties will increase in severity.

Immigration enforcement officers can and do carry out spot checks within employing organisations – and charge the employer if irregularities are discovered – far more frequently now than was the case in the past. Whilst, formerly, immigration enforcement officers might have focused on smaller companies on which to carry out compliance checks, this practice has now changed. Immigration enforcement officers are carrying out audits (often unannounced) on both small and large UK employers.

Employers are therefore well advised to take steps now to equip themselves to respond successfully to an audit from immigration enforcement officers. For an employer to defend itself successfully against a charge that it has been employing an illegal worker, the employer must be able to show that:

1. before the employee commenced work, the employer either checked and retained a copy of one original of a document listed in Table 8.1 or the employer checked and retained a copy of two original documents from either combination 1 or combination 2 listed in Table 8.2; and
2. the employee is the rightful holder of the documents. The employer should consider checking expiry dates and for consistency between different documents that are presented.

It is worth noting that the lists of acceptable documents set out above replaced alternative lists of acceptable documents in 2004. Rules introduced in 2004 mean that it is no longer lawful to rely upon a card or certificate issued by HMRC under the Construction Industry Scheme as evidence of that person's ability to work in the UK.

Table 8.1   Original documentation considered for checking

- A passport showing that the holder, or a person named in the passport as the child of the holder, is a British citizen or a citizen of the UK and Colonies having the right of abode in the UK.
- A passport or national identity card showing that the holder, or a person named in the passport as the child of the holder, is a national of the European Economic Area or Switzerland.
- A residence permit, registration certificate or document certifying or indicating permanent residence issued by the Home Office or Border and Immigration Agency to a national of a European Economic Area country or Switzerland.
- A permanent residence card issued by the Home Office or the Border and Immigration Agency to the family member if a national of a European Economic Area country or Switzerland.
- A Biometric Immigration Document issued by the Border and Immigration Agency to the holder which indicates that the person named in it is allowed to stay indefinitely in the UK, or has no time limit on their stay in the UK.
- A passport or other travel document endorsed to show that the holder is exempt from immigration control, is allowed to stay indefinitely in the UK, or has no time limit on their stay in the UK.
- An Immigration Status Document issued by the Home Office or the Border and Immigration Agency to the holder with an endorsement indicating that the person named in it is allowed to stay indefinitely in the UK or has no time limit on their stay in the UK, **when produced in combination with** an official document giving the person's permanent National Insurance Number and their name issued by a Government agency or a previous employer.
- A full birth certificate issued in the UK which includes the name(s) of at least one of the holder's parents, **when produced in combination with** an official document giving the person's permanent National Insurance Number and their name issued by a Government agency or a previous employer.
- A full adoption certificate issued in the UK which includes in the UK the name(s) of at least one of the holder's adoptive parents which produced in combination with an official document giving the person's permanent National Insurance Number and their name issued by a Government agency or a previous employer.
- A birth certificate issued in the Channel Islands, the Isle of Man or Ireland, **when produced in combination with** an official document giving the person's permanent National Insurance Number and their name issued by a Government agency or a previous employer.
- An adoption certificate issued in the Channel Islands, the Isle of Man or Ireland, when produced with an official document giving the person's permanent National Insurance Number and their name issued by a Government agency or a previous employer.
- A certificate of registration or naturalisation as a British citizen, when produced in combination with an official document giving the person's permanent National Insurance Number and their name issued by a Government agency or a previous employer.
- A letter issued by the Home Office or the Border and Immigration Agency to the holder which indicates that the person named in it is allowed to stay indefinitely in the UK when produced in combination with an official document giving the person's permanent National Insurance Number and their name issued by a Government agency or a previous employer.

Table 8.2   Combination 1 and combination 2 documentation

- A passport or travel document endorsed to show that the holder is allowed to stay in the UK and is allowed to do the type of work in question, provided that it does not require the issue of a work permit.

- A Biometric Immigration Document issued by the Border and Immigration Agency to the holder which indicates that the person named in it can stay in the UK and is allowed to do the work in question.

- A work permit or other approval to take employment issued by the Home Office or the Border and Immigration Agency **when produced in combination with** either a passport or another travel document endorsed to show the holder is allowed to do the work in question, or a letter issued by the Home Office or the Border and Immigration Agency to the holder or the employer or prospective employer confirming the same.

- A certificate of application issued by the Home Office or the Border and Immigration Agency to or for a family member of a national of European Economic Area country or Switzerland stating that the holder is permitted to take employment which is less than 6 months old **when produced in combination with** evidence of verification by the Border and Immigration Agency Employer Checking Service.

- A residence card or document issued by the Home Office or the Border and Immigration Agency to a family member of a national of a European Economic Area country or Switzerland.

- An Application Registration Card issued by the Home Office or the Border and Immigration Agency stating the holder is permitted to take employment, **when produced in combination with** evidence of verification by the Border and Immigration Agency Employer Checking Service.

- An Immigration Status Document issued by the Home Office or the Border and Immigration Agency to the holder with an endorsement indicating that the person named in it can stay in the UK, and is allowed to do the type of work in question, **when produced in combination with** an official document giving the person's permanent National Insurance Number and their name issued by a Government agency or a previous employer.

- A letter issued by the Home Office or the Border and Immigration Agency to the holder or the employer or prospective employer, which indicates that the person named in it can stay in the UK and is allowed to do the work in question **when produced in combination with** an official document giving the person's permanent National Insurance Number and their name issued by a Government agency or a previous employer.

Table 8.1 states that it is sufficient, for the purposes of compliance with the Act, for a prospective employee to demonstrate that he or she is a national of a member state of the European Economic Area (EEA) (i.e. citizens of all EU member states plus Iceland, Liechtenstein and Norway) or Switzerland. However, if an individual is a national of the Czech Republic, Estonia, Hungary, Latvia, Lithuania, Poland, Slovakia or Slovenia, in addition to proving that he or she is a member of the EU, he or she may also need to register under the Worker Registration Scheme (see below) in order to be able to work lawfully in the UK. This additional bureaucratic hurdle serves to make recruitment from these countries a little less attractive.

From 29 February 2008, section 13 of the Immigration, Asylum and Nationality Act 2006 amended the position in relation to document checks. Section 13 enables an employer to establish an 'excuse' against liability for payment of a civil penalty for employing an illegal migrant if it can show that before the employee started work it checked and copied certain original documents. If the person provides a document or documents from Table 8.1 this will establish an excuse for the duration of his or her employment. If a document or documents is produced from Table 8.2 that indicates that he or she only has limited leave to be in the UK, then checks should be repeated on that employee every 12 months until he or she produces documents indicating that he or she can remain permanently in the UK from Table 8.1.

Employers should be aware that if they are deemed to have known that the person was not permitted to work, they will not be entitled to an excuse. These new arrangements will only apply for those employees taken on after 29 February 2008.

If an employer is unsure about the status of a particular document that a prospective new recruit produces, or a particular stamp in a passport, it can contact the Home Office's Employer's helpline for assistance. The telephone number is 0845 010 6677. Another way of checking the document is to compare it to the pro forma immigration stamps which appear on the Home Office's website (www.ind.homeoffice.gov.uk).

Employers should make a note of when an individual's permission to remain in the UK expires and should diarise to check that the employee is still entitled to work in the UK on that date. It will be appreciated that there is a significant degree of active management required on the part of the employer's HR manager.

Employers should note that the obligation to carry out immigration checks only arises when the person working for them is, or is intended to be, their employee. Carrying out such checks when it is not intended that the worker is to be the employee of the employer can cause its own difficulties and may contribute to an argument that the worker was the employer's employee. This issue is considered in greater detail below.

An employer should take care when carrying out immigration checks to ensure that it does not discriminate against job candidates and employees on racial grounds (see further below).

8.2. ENTERING THE UK AS A FOREIGN NATIONAL

There is a variety of ways in which a foreign national can enter and work in the UK. The Home Office categorises foreign nationals by giving them different immigration 'labels'. It is important for employers to understand the significance of each label, because whilst some immigration categories entitle individuals to work in the UK, others do not. Some categories entitle individuals to work in the UK but subject to constraints.

If an employer wants to recruit a foreign national to work in the UK, the first step is to identify the most appropriate immigration category for the individual in question, based on the type of work that needs to be undertaken. The second step is to seek permission for the individual to enter or remain in the UK under that category. So, taking a prospective work permit holder as an example, employers should be aware of the need to obtain two tiers of permission before a non-EEA national can work for them in the UK:

1. The employer applies to Work Permits (UK) for permission (in the form of a work permit) to employ the person in a particular role; and
2. If this permission is granted, the employee applies to the Home Office (or, if they are not in the UK or are not permitted to switch from their current immigration category whilst within the UK, the appropriate British High Commission or British Embassy in their country of origin) for permission to enter and/ or remain in the UK as a work permit holder.

8.2.1. Step 1: Immigration categories

Set out below are the most common immigration categories that employers in the construction industry are likely to encounter.[1]

Worker registration scheme
(a) The majority of prospective employees bearing the passport of an EEA country is entitled to live and work in the UK without first obtaining permission to do so from the Home Office. However, this is not the case for nationals from the following EEA countries:
   (i)   the Czech Republic;
   (ii)   Estonia;
   (iii) Hungary;
   (iv)   Latvia;
   (v)   Lithuania;
   (vi)   Poland;
   (vii) Slovakia; and
   (viii) Slovenia.

   If nationals from one of the EU countries listed above find a job in the UK and wish to work for their employer for more than one month, they are required to apply for registration with the Home Office under the 'Worker Registration Scheme' as soon as they find work. Once such workers have been working legally in the UK for 12 months, they no longer need to register under the Scheme and will have full rights of free movement and employment.

(b) The purpose of the Worker Registration Scheme is to monitor the impact on the labour market of workers arriving in the UK from these particular countries. The numbers of such workers will be monitored as well as their location and the industries in which they are employed.

(c) Applications for registration under the Scheme are the responsibility of the individual. However, when applying for registration, the individual will need a letter on company paper confirming the date on which he or she began working.

Employers will be responsible for ensuring that they are authorised to employ an individual from one of these eight countries. Subject to first complying with the checks required by the Act, an employer will be so authorised during the first month of the individual's work. If the individual applies, during that first month, for a registration certificate then the employer will continue to be authorised until the application is decided. If a registration certificate is issued, an employer will continue to be authorised to employ that person.

Work permit holder

(a) The work permit scheme enables UK-based employers to recruit or bring employees from outside the EEA to work in the UK. The individual must work for the employer making the application. Applications are made to a division of the Home Office known as Work Permits (UK).

(b) Strict rules apply to work permit applications; in most cases the employee will need to have a UK degree-level qualification in order to be considered for a work permit. Additionally, unless the position which the prospective employee is intended to fill is regarded by Work Permits (UK) as being a 'shortage occupation' (for example, doctors or qualified nurses), the employer will also have to show that it has advertised the role within the EEA and that this search has shown that there are no EEA nationals who are suitable to undertake the job. This is usually evidenced by way of an unsuccessful advertising and recruitment campaign, which itself must fulfil Work Permits (UK)'s specifications.

(c) If an employer of a non-EEA national has obtained a work permit for him or her to work in another EEA country, that work permit does not automatically transfer to the UK if the employer chooses to second the employee to the UK. In *Van der Elst* the European Court decided that an employer had the freedom to move such employees around Europe, in accordance with the needs of the employer's business. However, this right does not arise automatically – a further application to the Home Office is needed in such circumstances. The relevant Home Office procedure states that, under the Van der Elst principle, a non-EEA national working for an EEA employer in another member state of the EEA is allowed to provide services in the UK without the need to obtain a work permit, provided the employee:

(i) is lawfully resident in the EEA member state in which his or her employer is established;

(ii) has been lawfully and habitually employed by his or her employer (for at least 12 months) in a member state of the EEA;

(iii) intends to provide a service in the UK on a temporary basis; and

(iv) does not intend to take up other employment in the UK and intends to leave the UK at the end of the period.

Although the worker who qualifies to work in the UK under this principle will not be required to obtain a work permit, he or she will still need to apply to the Home Office for a visa. The Van der Elst visa is, however, sometimes more difficult and time-consuming to obtain than a standard local work permit under UK law.

Business visitor

(a) If an employer wishes to invite an individual to the UK to attend meetings and briefings, negotiate or enter into contracts with UK businesses (but not the general public) to buy or sell goods or services, that individual may enter the UK for up to six months as a 'business visitor'.

(b) A business visitor must satisfy several conditions, which include an intention to leave the UK at the end of the visit and an ability to maintain and accommodate him or herself without the need to be supported out of public funds. Most importantly, a business visitor does not have permission to carry out 'work' in the UK and therefore must not be, or become, an employee of the UK employer (see Chapter 2 in relation to employment status).

Student

(a) Non-EEA nationals who have permission to enter the UK as students are entitled to take up to 20 hours' paid employment per week during term time. It will be the responsibility of the employer to ensure that these limits are not breached.

(b) During university holidays, the 20-hour per week cap on taking paid employment is removed for students. It will be the responsibility of the employer to obtain written confirmation from the university or college attended by the student as to the dates of the school holidays.

Highly skilled migrant

(a) The Highly Skilled Migrant Programme enables those who can score a requisite number of points (based on various factors such as their previous earnings and existing qualifications) to come into the UK to work or look for work. Those given entry under the programme are also able to set up their own businesses in the UK, bring their families here and (ultimately) apply for settlement.

Working holidaymaker

(a) Nationals of Commonwealth countries aged between 17 and 30 (inclusive) may apply to the Home Office for permission to enter and remain in the UK for a period of up to two years as working holidaymakers.

(b) Until recently, working holidaymakers were entitled to spend the entire two-year period in paid employment in the UK. However, this permission has recently been reduced so that working holiday-makers are only entitled to spend 50% of their stay in the UK in paid employment. In addition to carrying out the immigration checks set out above, employers considering employing working holidaymakers are therefore obliged to make enquiries as to the amount of time the person has spent working in the UK at the time they take them on.

Self-employed foreign national

(a) An EC Association Agreement exists which allows Bulgarian nationals the right to enter the UK and pursue economic activities in a self-employed capacity (the Scheme). In May 2004, amid alle-gations of abuse of the Scheme, applications from the self-employed were suspended pending an investigation by the Home Office.

(b) The right of establishment under the Scheme relates only to self-employment. The rules are clear that this 'should not amount to concealed employment'. There is no identifiable sole determining factor for distinguishing employment from self-employment but there is a number of indicative factors. When trying to establish an individual's status, these factors should first be considered in turn in light of the circumstances of the applicant. The whole pic-ture should then be examined to establish whether the overall effect indicates a person who is employed or who is self-employed. The factors indicating self-employment or otherwise are similar to the factors set out in Chapter 2.

GATS permit
(a) Under the GATS scheme, the Home Office will consider applications for permits in respect of individuals to work in the UK on a service contract awarded to their overseas employer by a UK-based organisation. The overseas employer must not have a presence in the EU and the contract must be awarded, on the basis of economic need, through an open tendering process (or by some other means which demonstrates that the contract is *bona fide*). Relevant sectors in respect of which permits are awarded include 'engineering services', and 'technical testing and analysis services'.

(b) Permission for employment in the UK is granted on the condition that there is an incentive for the individual to leave the UK once the work is complete and, in any event, at the end of a maximum of three months in any 12-month period. The individual should have spent a minimum of 12 months in the employment of the overseas employer before the application is made. The individual must also have obtained recognised degree-level qualifications and have at least three years' professional experience in the sector.

8.2.2. Step 2: Obtaining entry clearance to the UK/permission to remain in the UK

If the individual is an EEA national
(a) If the individual is a national of the European Union (EU) or a national of Iceland, Liechtenstein or Norway (members of the EEA but not the EU) or Switzerland, EU law gives him or her the right to live and work in the UK. There is no need to obtain entry clearance from a British Diplomatic Post overseas prior to travelling. Individuals will have a right of residence in the UK if they are EEA or Swiss nationals and they are working. Alternatively, if they are not working but they have enough money to support themselves throughout their stay without help from public funds, they will also have a right of residence.

(b) Individuals who have a right of residence do not need to get a residence permit or register with the police. Individuals can apply for a residence permit if they so desire, but this simply confirms that they have the right to live in the UK under EU law. Individuals do need to apply for a residence permit if their family members want to apply for a residence document or if the individual wishes to qualify for permanent residence.

If the individual is a non-EEA national
(a) Non-EEA nationals will normally require a work permit to enter the UK for the purpose of employment (unless they can fit into any of the other immigration categories). If a work permit is

granted to the employer, each individual will have to apply, on the strength of the permit granted to the employer, to the appropriate British Diplomatic Post in his or her country of origin for permission to enter and remain in the UK as a work permit holder.

(b) If the person is currently in the UK under another immigration category (or, importantly, as a work permit holder for another employer), once permission has been gained from Work Permits (UK) the individual may, in certain circumstances, be able to apply to the Home Office to 'switch' immigration categories. The ability to switch from one immigration category to another whilst remaining in the UK does not apply to all immigration categories.

(c) If the non-EEA national wishes to work in the UK under any of the other immigration categories mentioned above, he or she will have to apply for permission to enter and remain in the UK under that particular category to:

   (i)   (if they are abroad or are not entitled to switch between the two immigration categories in question) the relevant British Diplomatic Post overseas; or

   (ii) (if they are in the UK and are entitled to switch between the two immigration categories in question) the Home Office.

8.3. EMPLOYMENT STATUS

When engaging the services of a non-EEA national, the employer should consider the impact of the worker's employment status on the business and on its duties to carry out immigration checks. For example, if the worker is classed as an 'employee' of the employer, he or she will be entitled not to be unfairly dismissed. If the worker is not the 'employee' of the employer, the duty to carry out checks under the Asylum and Immigration Act 1996 (the Act) does not arise. In fact, employers who are not intending that workers should be regarded in law as their employees should take care to ensure that the obligations under the Act are undertaken by the worker's 'employer' – whether this be the agency supplying the worker or the worker's service company. The employer should seek comfort that the checks required under the Act have been carried out effectively by the entity who has the duty to carry them out, by requesting copies of the paperwork obtained from the individual workers.

8.4. DISCRIMINATION AND IMMIGRATION

Whilst the onus is on an employer to carry out the requisite immigration checks, care must be taken to ensure that non-EEA job candidates and employees are not discriminated against in the process.

Under the Race Relations Act 1976 it is unlawful for an employer to discriminate against job candidates and employees on the grounds of their race, colour, ethnic or national origin. Refusing to consider a job candidate who looks or sounds foreign or requiring them to produce different documentation to job candidates who look or sound British could amount to unlawful race discrimination. If an employer is found to have done this, it could face discrimination claims and be ordered to pay compensation, on which there is no statutory limit.

The Home Office provides guidance in relation to this issue on its website (www.ind. homeoffice.gov.uk/ind/en/home/0/preventing_illegal/ avoiding_racial_discrimination.html) and the Commission for Racial Equality has published guidance: *The Asylum and Immigration Act 1996: Implications for Racial Equality*. The over-riding principle which emerges is that businesses should ensure that they treat all job candidates identically, regardless of ethnic origin. In practical terms, this means that all new starters should, as a matter of course, be asked to produce the requisite numbers of documents listed above (from either Table 8.1 or Table 8.2) on their first day of employment. Offers of employment should always be made conditional upon (amongst other things) satisfactory completion of these immigration checks.

8.5. THE IMMIGRATION, NATIONALITY AND ASYLUM BILL

The Immigration, Asylum and Nationality Act received Royal assent in March 2006. However, at the time of publication some sections of the Act are not yet in force. The Act is part of the on-going implementation of the government's five-year strategy on immigration and asylum, 'Controlling our borders: Making migration work for Britain' published in February 2005. The aim of the Act is to produce tighter immigration controls.

The Bill includes measures to:

(a) **Strengthen the UK's borders**
    (i) Allowing data sharing between border agencies as part of the transformation of our border control through the e-Borders programme – under section 36 (not yet in force). The Immigration Service, Police and HM Revenue & Customs will be able to access passenger information from carriers more easily, helping them identify individuals who may present a risk to security or immigration control.
    (ii) Supporting the global roll-out of fingerprinting visa applicants by giving powers to Immigration Officers to verify identity against biometrics contained in travel documents – under section 27.

(b) **Tackle illegal working**
    (i)   Introducing a new civil penalties scheme for employers intro-ducing fines of up to £2000 per illegal employee and a possible two-year custodial sentence and unlimited fine for those found knowingly to use or exploit illegal workers – under section 21.

(c) **Restrict appeals**
    (i)   Limiting rights of appeal for those refused entry to the UK to work or study and restricting rights of appeal in family visit cases to close family only, emphasising that entry to the UK for managed migration purposes is a privilege and not a right – under section 4 (not yet in force) and section 6 (now in force).

8.6. CONCLUSION

The Home Office dictates changes to immigration procedures and policies in line with the perceived needs of the UK's economy. The Home Office also processes applications received from employers and individuals in accordance with the perceived importance of the application. Consequently, not only can immigration laws change from time to time, but procedures can change very rapidly and there is a consequent need for employers to keep abreast of developments.

NOTE

1. The government is intending to implement a new immigration strategy to commence in March 2008. The system is set within a five tier framework, the idea of which is to underpin all routes of entry into the UK – consolidating approximately 80 routes to just five. This is unlikely to affect the worker registration scheme, but the reader should be aware that all other categories described in section 8.2.1 are likely to be subject to some revision.

CHAPTER 9

TUPE and the construction industry

The Transfer of Undertakings (Protection of Employment) Regulations 2006,[1] commonly known by the acronym TUPE, are of major importance to employers in the construction industry. They raise issues where:

- a business is transferred (for example, where the business of one contractor is sold to another or where a contractor takes on a number of building contracts from the receiver of an insolvent contractor); or
- where responsibility for the provision of services changes from one contractor to another (for example, where a local authority outsources jobbing maintenance work in its estate of council houses, or where a contractor wins a retender for the maintenance of a part of the railway network).

The increase in Private Finance Initiative/Public Private Partnerships (PFI/PPP) projects, facilities management and outsourcing contracts within the industry has resulted in construction companies having to deal with TUPE issues with increasing frequency. Issues relating to changes of service provider are encountered with particular regularity.

It is important to be able to predict when TUPE will apply and what the consequences of TUPE will be, in order that an appropriate bid may be made for an acquisition target or that contracts for the provision of services can be appropriately priced. It is because the circumstances in which TUPE will apply have been so difficult to predict and the legal principles so confused that this area of employment law has become notorious. The 2006 revision of TUPE represents an attempt to eradicate some of these uncertainties; in this respect it has been partially successful but many pitfalls remain.

9.1. GENERAL PRINCIPLES

TUPE implements the provisions of the European Union Directive,[2] in UK law, '*on the approximation of the laws of Member States relating to the safeguarding of employee rights in the event of transfers of undertakings between businesses or parts of a business*', which is more commonly known as the Acquired Rights Directive (the Directive). The policy objective behind the Directive is to protect the rights of employees who work in an 'undertaking' (typically a business or the provision of a service) which is being transferred or where there is a change of a service provider.

Where TUPE applies, its implications may be summarised as follows:

- The contracts of employment of those employees employed in the undertaking immediately before the transfer are transferred by operation of law to the purchaser of the business or to the incoming service provider, as if the transferee employer had always been the employer.
- Not only does the transferee employer inherit the contracts of employment of the transferring employees, but also the extent to which these contracts may be changed (even with the consent of all the parties) is strictly limited.
- All rights, duties and liabilities of the transferor employer arising under or in connection with the transferring contracts of employment are transferred to the transferee employer (subject to certain limited exceptions). The transferee employer becomes liable for the acts and omissions of the transferor employer, such as arrears of wages or acts of unlawful discrimination.
- Any dismissal of an employee who is affected by the transfer of an undertaking for a reason connected with the transfer will be *automatically* unfair, unless the dismissal was for an 'economic, technical or organisational reason entailing a change in the workforce'.
- An obligation arises to inform and, in certain, circumstances to consult with the appropriate representatives of the employees who may be affected by the transfer of the undertaking.
- The transferor employer must, at least 14 days before the transfer, provide to the transferee employer certain employee liability information in writing.
- Collective agreements and union recognition may transfer.

9.2.   WHEN DOES TUPE APPLY?

Given that if TUPE applies, a number of important employment consequences follow, it is crucial to establish when TUPE applies and when it does not. Since the 2001 Regulations, there have been two tests. The generally accepted test of whether there is a transfer of an undertaking is whether *'what has been [transferred] is an economic entity which is still in existence [after the transfer], and this will be apparent from the fact that its operation is actually being continued or has been taken over by the new employer, with the same economic or similar activities'*.[3] Alternatively, the second test is whether there has been a 'service provision change', as defined?

The 'economic entity' test is not an easy test to apply. It is easy to identify an acquisition of a self-standing business as an economic entity capable of a TUPE transfer. Conversely, the mere transfer of some items of plant and machinery is not likely, of itself, to constitute an economic entity. Just where the border is crossed between these two extremes, however, is often unclear.

The question of whether a given set of circumstances amounts to a transfer of an economic entity can only be answered after consideration of all the features of the activity which are being transferred. No one factor is likely to be decisive. Amongst the factors to be taken into account in this determination are:

- the nature of the activity which is the subject of the transfer;
- whether tangible assets such as buildings and movable property are to be transferred;
- whether intangible assets are to be transferred, and the extent of their value;
- whether or not the majority of the employees is to be taken on by the transferee employer post transfer;
- whether or not the transferor employer's customers are to be transferred;
- the degree of similarity between the activities carried on before and after the transfer; and
- the period, if any, for which activities are to be suspended on or after the transfer.[4]

It is important to note, in the context of the transfer of construction work, that the transfer of a contract that merely involved the completion of snagging works was held not to be a transfer of a stable economic entity and therefore TUPE did not apply.[5] In that case, the activity concerned was the completion of a subcontract for joinery work on a construction project, the original sub-contractor having defaulted. There was held not to be a TUPE transfer to the incoming sub-contractor because, come the end of the building project, the undertaking of providing joinery services was to cease. The full extent of the implications of this judgment in the context of construction projects has yet to be determined.

In the majority of business acquisitions, TUPE will apply because the purchaser of the business is interested in acquiring the 'economic entity' with a view to continuing the enterprise. Where the activity is the delivery of services, however, the position is often less clear.

It was for this reason that the 2006 revision of TUPE attempted to achieve greater clarity in this area.[6] The new law has introduced a broad set of provisions which apply in cases of service provision change, which will mean that henceforth most changes of service provision will be caught by TUPE.

A 'service provision change' is defined as where 'activities' are out-sourced, insourced or where responsibility passes from one contractor to another (so called 'second generation' outsourcing). For the provisions of TUPE to apply, there must have been – immediately before the service provision change – an organised grouping of employees, situated in Great Britain, which has as its principal purpose the carrying out of activities on behalf of the client. The intention must be that, after the change, the activities are carried out by the transferee employer other than in connection with a single specific event or a short-term task. It will be appreciated that much turns on the way in which a service is organised. Take, for example, the situation where a local authority has a group of maintenance workers who undertake maintenance work on a large council estate, based at a depot near the estate. If those services are transferred, there will inevitably be a TUPE transfer. Consider, however, a situation where, in the five years until retender, the successful private sector contractor seeks and wins other maintenance contracts, which are serviced out of the same depot. On retender, much would depend on the extent of the diversification. It is not fatal that the depot no longer focuses solely on the maintenance work guaranteed by the council estate. However, if the extent of the diversification means that the council estate work can no longer be said to be 'the principal purpose' of the depot, there may not be a TUPE transfer.

In many cases there will not be a straightforward transfer of service providers. There may be circumstances where one set of services is gradually run down, with replacement services being phased in; or there may be a replacement of one service provider with a panel of contractors operating under framework contracts. These circumstances do not fit easily into the rules of TUPE, neither do circumstances where the specification of the services is changed. There is only a limited amount of guidance available in these areas and it is down to the employment tribunals (with the benefit of hindsight) to seek to apply these basic principles to circumstances which are often complex.

There may be circumstances where, notwithstanding that there is no transfer for the purpose of the service change provisions, there may still be a transfer of an undertaking under the general rules regarding the transfer of an undertaking, but these will be few and far between.

Commercial uncertainty has been the inevitable result of a lack of clarity in the law. Notwithstanding the 2006 revisions to the law, the position will still be unclear in many cases. There is a risk that an incoming contractor may suffer an unforeseen transfer of employees. Cost implications are likely to include redundancy and unfair dismissal liabilities or payroll overheads in excess of what might otherwise have been incurred due to the transfer of historic liabilities. The contractor pricing a contract for the provision of services will invariably make assumptions for commercial purposes. It is advisable to underpin those assumptions wherever possible – for example by pricing the risk of a TUPE transfer into a tender for the provision of services or by allocating TUPE risks within a contract for the sale and purchase of a business by the use of warranties and indemnities. A properly drafted contract may allow scope for 'hedging' against the vagaries of the law in this area. Likewise, the TUPE risks on exit should be anticipated and priced for or be laid off in the contract.

9.3. WHO TRANSFERS?

Those employees who are employed in the undertaking or the part of an undertaking immediately before the transfer will become employees of the transferee. Although the transfer takes place automatically by operation of law, there is plenty of scope for the transferor to redeploy employees so as to bring them within or take them out of the scope of TUPE.

Should a transferor employer wish to retain the services of an employee who is earmarked for transfer, he could do so by redeploying him so that he is not employed immediately before the transfer in the undertaking which is the subject of the transfer. The converse, a practice known colloquially as 'dumping', involves the transferor employer moving employees into the undertaking at the eleventh hour so that the employees are technically employed in the undertaking which transfers immediately before the transfer, and become employees of the transferee employer. Typically, this practice results in the transferee employer inheriting an overmanned workforce and/or poor-quality employees.

While the courts and tribunals have expressed a distaste for such practices, it is often difficult for a transferee employer to spot and the language of TUPE makes it almost impossible for the transferee employer to seek redress on legal grounds.

A further danger for transferee employers, which hangs on the term 'immediately before', surrounds dismissals prior to the transfer. The courts have held[7] that a dismissal which cannot be said to have taken place immediately before the transfer, in the literal sense of the phrase, but which was occasioned by reason of the transfer (for example, dismissals to make an overmanned business more attractive to a potential purchaser) will be deemed to have been made 'immediately before the transfer' and hence the liabilities associated with these dismissals will transfer to the transferee employee.

Whether an employee can be said to be employed in the undertaking is another area of difficulty, particularly where only a part of an undertaking is being transferred. Employees often will work some of their time on one project and the rest of their time elsewhere within the employer's business. Only those employees who are 'assigned' to the undertaking or part of an undertaking which is being transferred will transfer to the transferee employer.[8]

The 2006 revision of TUPE did not seek to address this complex issue.

Take, for example, a situation where a maintenance contractor is responsible for providing a variety of services to the building of a certain client (Client A). The contractor services those buildings from its local depot, which also services a variety of other clients. Client A puts the contract out to retender and the contractor loses. As a consequence, the contractor loses a significant volume of work for the particular depot. If the appointment of a new contractor by Client A amounts to a TUPE transfer, the question to be asked is, which employees of the outgoing contractor become employees of the incoming contractor? If a given employee is assigned to work exclusively or principally for Client A, the position is clear. If, however, an employee is not assigned exclusively to the work of Client A, but rather works for a variety of different clients including Client A, at different times, to varying degrees, potentially that employee may not transfer and may leave the outgoing contractor with a redundancy liability if it has no other work on which to deploy him. In practice, the assignment test has been stretched to recognise that someone who spends a significant proportion of his time on the work of Client A amongst a range of other clients may be considered to have been assigned to the transferring service contract. Just what proportion of his time and over what period of time he must have spent on work for Client A to qualify as 'assigned' is not clear. However, the greater the proportion of time, the greater the likelihood that the employee will transfer. Ordinarily an employee must have worked at least 50% of his time on the transferring service contract. The uncertainty surrounding the issue of assignment means that it is often advisable for incoming and outgoing contractors to negotiate and settle which employees are assigned and therefore transfer and which do not; failure to do so can result in an unpredictable dispute before an employment tribunal.

A further point to bear in mind is that in order to transfer, the worker must be an employee (as opposed to an independent contractor) of the transferor. Those who perform services under a contract for services are specifically excluded.

In order to transfer, the worker must be an employee of the transferor as opposed to any other party. A large construction company will typically have a substantial number of subsidiary companies. Often all the employees within the group will be employed by one service company. Should a subsidiary decide to sell or outsource its business or a part of its business, it is likely that there will be no employees employed by the transferor subsidiary company in the transferring business – hence the employees who ordinarily work in that business do not fall within the protection of TUPE. Much as the courts dislike this loophole,[9] it is there to be exploited.

9.4. CAN EMPLOYEES REFUSE TO TRANSFER?

Employees who would otherwise transfer have the right to opt out of the transfer. If they do so, however,[10] their employment will terminate without giving rise to a right to claim a redundancy payment or that they have been unfairly dismissed. As there is no transfer, no other employment liabilities (such as non-payment of wages) in respect of that employee will transfer to the transferee employer.

It has been held that an employee's objection to being transferred can be conveyed by word or deed.[11] It was a question of fact in each case whether the employee's state of mind amounted to a withholding of consent to the transfer and whether the state of mind was brought to the attention of the transferor employer.

Where an employee believes that there has been a repudiatory breach of contract he may claim constructive dismissal. Alternatively, where the transfer results in a substantial change to an employee's terms and conditions, the employee may treat his employment as having ended and the tribunal will consider whether there is an unfair dismissal.[12]

One way in which attempts are frequently made to circumvent the effects of TUPE is by seconding an employee who would otherwise have transferred, the purpose of the secondment being to retain the opportunity to recall the employee at some time after the transfer. Such tactics have only a limited chance of success and should be approached with caution.[13]

9.5. TRANSFER OF TERMS AND CONDITIONS

TUPE provides[14] that 'all the transferor's rights, powers, duties and liabilities under or in connection with the transferring employee's contract of employment are transferred to the transferee'.

This all-embracing concept includes:

- rights under the contract of employment;
- statutory rights; and
- continuity of employment.

Rights which transfer include:

(a) *Terms and Conditions*: Employees become employees of the trans-feree on the same terms and conditions. To a large extent, it is as if a contract of employment has been pulled from the personnel records and the name of the transferor employer changed to the transferee employer. There is some debate as to whether a term must be expressly contractual to transfer. It would appear that non-contractual provisions can transfer – but they would clearly have the same non-contractual effect as regards the transferee.

(b) *Status*: The employment relationship is transferred as if the employee had always been employed by the transferee. Hence, any employment benefits that relate to the employee's status would also transfer – for example, holiday entitlement which is calculated by length of service would be calculated on the basis of continuity of service stretching back before the transfer. Equally, seniority is capable transferring.

(c) *Arrears of pay and other liabilities*: As there is a transfer of the employment relationship and of all associated liabilities, any con-tractual arrears will transfer. For example, if there are arrears of pay, outstanding expenses or accrued benefits, such as holiday pay, these will all transfer. Needless to say, it is important for the purchaser of a business to either quantify these outstanding liabilities and to anticipate them when settling on a purchase price or to ensure the transferor employer provides an indemnity for such liabilities. Ideally, both steps should be taken although the latter will only be appropriate if the transferor is credit worthy for the indemnity. For an incoming contractor with no contract between it and the former provider of services, the position will not be so straightfor-ward although the incoming contractor may be able to secure some protection through its contract with the client.

(d) *Statutory claim*: Statutory rights will transfer in tandem with the transfer of the employee's terms and conditions. This will mean, for example, that an employee who has been employed by the trans-feree for only a matter of months may have the right to bring a claim for unfair dismissal against the transferee employer shortly after the transfer because of the aggregation of his pre-transfer service. The date of commencement of continuous service will be the date that applied in relation to employment with the transferor employer.

(e) *Restrictive covenants*: As contract terms, restrictive covenants will transfer. However, the extent to which they are appropriate to protect the transferee employer's legitimate business interests must be reviewed by the transferee employer. The transferor employer should also bear in mind that he will lose the protection of restrictive covenants, for the benefit of the covenants will trans-fer to become a contractual benefit for the transferee employer.

(f) *]Bonuses, profit sharing and share options*: These rights are capable of transferring as a matter of theory, but in practice the conditions that attach to bonuses and profit sharing schemes and the rules of share option schemes will generally be drafted so that the right to participate in such schemes ceases to exist upon the employee ceasing to be employed by the transferee employer. Furthermore, the criteria for the award of bonuses will have changed by reason of the transfer. In order to avoid a breach of contract, the transferee employer may have to put into place benefits of equivalent value.

(g) *Industrial injuries*: An industrial injury claim will transfer. Hence, the transferee could find itself liable for substantial claims where, for example, employees were exposed, pre transfer, to a harmful working environment. Particular attention should be given by the transferee employer to insurance cover in respect of such claims, which may have arisen at the time when the transferee did not have insurance in place in respect of these employees. There is case-law to suggest that in these circumstances reliance may be placed on the transferor's insurance.[15] Where there is no legal obligation to put insurance in place (largely in the public sector) the transferor and the transferee are liable on a joint and several basis.[16]

The following do not transfer:

(a) *Pensions*: Certain rights in relation to occupational pension schemes are specifically excluded from transfer pursuant to TUPE.[17] The following points, however, should be born in mind:
  • It is only rights in relation to occupational pension schemes that do not transfer. If, for example, there was a clause in an employee's contract of employment whereby his employer was obliged to pay 5% of salary into a personal pension plan on behalf of that employee, then such a right would not be a right in relation to an occupational pension scheme and would transfer.
  • It is only the provisions of an occupational pension scheme that relate to old age, invalidity or survivors that will not transfer. If, for example, there is a severance benefit scheme built into the pension scheme, then this would transfer. TUPE was written in this way because the Civil Service Pension Scheme, for example, contains a contractual redundancy scheme. The most spectacular example of this limitation is the case of *Beckmann* v. *Dynamco Whicheloe Macfarlane*. Mrs Beckmann's terms and conditions derived from her employment within the National Health Service prior to transfer. She had been a member of the NHS Pension Scheme, which contains an entitlement in the event of dismissal prior to normal retirement in the form of an immediate pension and compensation. Mrs Beckmann was made redundant by the

transferee. The European Court held that early retirement benefits cannot be described as 'old-age benefits' for the purposes of the pensions exception:

> 'It is only benefits paid from the time when an employee reaches the end of his normal working life as laid down by the general structure of the pension scheme in question, and not benefits such as those in point in the main proceedings (dismissal for redundancy), that can be classified as old-age benefits, even if they are calculated by reference to the rules for calculating normal pension benefits.'

The passage quoted above suggests that any benefits payable prior to the normal retirement date will fall outside the exception, not just those arising on redundancy. This was confirmed when the *Beckmann* decision was considered and followed in *Martin* v. *South Bank University*. Given that a large proportion of pension schemes provide members with the right to an early retirement pension as of right, these decisions caused widespread alarm, bearing in mind that a transferee could now be held responsible to provide an early retirement pension but without any corresponding right to receive a transfer of the assets that would have been built up in the transferor's pension scheme to meet this liability. Just what entitlements employees have in the circumstances and what obligations lie upon the parties to the transfer and on the trustees of the scheme of which the employees were formerly active members remains unclear following these two decisions of the European Court.

A further limitation on the now much reduced scope of the pensions exception was introduced by the Pensions Act 2004. A transferee now has a modified obligation to provide pension benefits following a TUPE transfer. The obligation is triggered by the answer to the question of whether the transferor provided access to an occupational pension scheme (or would have done so but for a deliberate attempt to avoid these provisions). If it did, then those transferring employees who were members of the scheme, were eligible to be members or were in a waiting period to become eligible to become a member will have a right to be provided with certain pension benefits post transfer. These will not be an entitlement to participate in a broadly comparable pension scheme, the benchmark for public to private-sector transfers. Instead, the transferee will be obliged to provide a certain minimum standard of pension benefits, subject to the right of the transferee and the employee to agree whatever pension terms they wish (including the right to opt out of the right to any pension benefits at all) at any time post transfer, pursuant to section 258(6) of the Pensions Act 2004. There is (unlike the general principle elsewhere within TUPE) no attempt to replicate the level of benefit received pre transfer. Hence the employee may be better off or worse off following the transfer; the level of benefits enjoyed prior to the transfer is of no consequence in relation to his rights following the transfer.

Once the obligation is triggered the transferee may choose either to provide membership of a defined benefits scheme (which must meet certain minimum standards) or of a money purchase scheme, which could be a stakeholder scheme. In the case of the latter, the employer contribution will be a matching contribution of up to 6% of the employee's basic pay.

If the transferee opts for the defined benefit route, the minimum standard with which that scheme must comply is either:

(a) the statutory reference scheme test for contracting out purposes; or

(b) the test set out in the Transfer of Employment (Pension Protection) Regulations 2005, whereby the value of the benefits accruing under the scheme each year must be at least 6% of the employee's pensionable pay, excluding the value of the employee contributions. If employees are required to make contributions, these must not exceed 6% of pensionable salary. Alternatively, the employer must make matching contributions of up to 6% of the employee's basic pay.

The date on which the obligations arise will either be the date of the relevant transfer for the purposes of TUPE or the date on which the employee reaches the end of the waiting period.

In the case of transfers out of the public sector, government guidance to public authorities is to require the transferee to commit, as a matter of contract, to provide a higher level of pension benefits as compared to those which would otherwise be provided pursuant to the ordinary principles under TUPE. Hence the common label 'TUPE Plus' which attaches to these enhanced obligations.

Assuming that the public authority places TUPE Plus pension obligations on the transferee as a contractual burden, the two key principles in 'A Fair Deal for Staff Pensions' are:

(a) that staff should continue to have access post transfer to a good-quality occupational pension scheme in respect of future service;

(b) that staff should be given options for handling the accrued benefits which they have already earned.

The benchmark for the provision of pension benefits going forward is a pension scheme which is 'broadly comparable' to the public sector pension scheme in which the employees participated pre transfer. Before the public authority will be prepared to enter into a contract which will result in a TUPE transfer, they will ordinarily want to see a 'pensions passport' – that is to say a certificate of broad comparability from the Government Actuary's Department, following scrutiny of the transferee's scheme.

(b) *Criminal liability*

(c) *Vicarious liability*: whereby the employer becomes liable for the acts of the employee done in the course of his employment, does not transfer.

9.6. CHANGING TERMS AND CONDITIONS POST TRANSFER

Transferee employers will often wish to harmonise the employment contracts of the transferring employees with those of their existing workforce and will often wish to change terms and conditions to tie performance more closely to remuneration.

However, although it is possible to change terms and conditions as a matter of general law, such variations are restricted when they take place in connection with a TUPE transfer.

Changes will be void if the sole or principal reason for the variation is the transfer itself. A change where the sole or principal reason for the variation is a reason connected with the transfer will be void unless that reason is an economic, technical or organisational reason (ETO reason) entailing changes in the workforce. Changes unconnected with the transfer will be permissible.

It can be very difficult to establish an ETO reason. Although there may be an apparent 'economic', 'technical' or 'organisational' reason for the change, there must also be a change in the workforce as a consequence, which means a change in the number or functions of the workforce taken as a whole.

Unfortunately, the distinction between a reason connected to a transfer and the case where the transfer itself is the reason is far from clear. A common question is how long does a transferee employer have to wait to show that a change is no longer connected with the transfer? Is it merely a question of time? What factors are determinative of this issue? On this point, considerable confusion still exists as the matter, according to the House of Lords,[18] must be determined by the employment tribunal based on the particular circumstances of the case. Practically, it appears that employers seeking to harmonise their employees' terms and conditions are only able to do so to the extent that each party is prepared to adhere to the bargain. Unfortunately, the employees are able to re-open their contracts of employment after the alleged variation and limitation laws allow contract-based claims to be brought up to six years later. Employers, when considering harmonisation, should take steps to establish that the reasons for the variation are not connected to the transfer. For example, they could argue that the variations were due to advances in technology; or in line with the employer's continuing group-wide review of all its contracts. Unfortunately, however ingenious these arguments may be, it must be recognised that an employment tribunal or court may still find that the underlying reason was the transfer and that the variations are therefore void. Dismissed and re-employment on the new terms is preferable, to deal with this difficulty, but such a manoeuvre brings problems of its own.

9.7. TRANSFER-CONNECTED DISMISSALS

Dismissals connected with a transfer are subject to the presumption that they are automatically unfair unless they are for an economic, technical or organisational reason entailing a change in the workforce. Even if a dismissal is not subject to the presumption that it is unfair, it may nevertheless be found to be unfair under general principles.

If a dismissal is found to be unfair, liability will transfer to the transferee who will be liable for any unfair dismissal award. It is therefore essential for the transferee to consider before dismissing any employees:

1. whether the reason for dismissal is connected with the transfer;
2. if so, is the ETO defence available; and
3. if so, will the dismissal be fair in any event?

It has been held[19] that for an employer to claim an ETO defence, it must show that it plans to change the numbers or functions of the employees looked at as a whole. An ETO defence will not be available if a planned harmonisation does not involve changes in numbers or functions of the workforce as it will not 'entail changes in the workforce'. However, a redundancy programme following a transfer will generally provide a transferee employer with an ETO defence since it involves a reduction in the numbers of employees required to carry out work of a particular kind.

As stated above, if the transferee is able to show an ETO defence or if the dismissal was not connected to the transfer, the general principles of fairness apply.[20] If there are redundancies to be made, the transferee must follow a fair procedure in adequately consulting with the employees (and their representatives) and selecting fairly the employees to be dismissed. With this in mind, a transferee should be particularly concerned to clarify whether it has inherited a contractual redundancy procedure from the transferor which may have to be followed, as well as whether there are any enhanced redundancy terms which transfer.

9.8. INFORMATION AND CONSULTATION

TUPE imposes obligations on both the transferor and the transferee employer to inform and, in most circumstances, to consult with representatives of the employees who may be affected by the transfer in relation to the proposed transfer and its implications. The consultation must be meaningful, must seek to achieve agreement and must take place in 'good time' before the transfer to allow for proper consultation.

Failure to inform or to consult in accordance with Regulation 13 of TUPE can result in protective awards being payable to each employee in respect of where there is a failure, which can be as high as 13 weeks' pay for each employee.

Checklist of transferor's responsibilities to inform and consult under Regulations 13 and 16 of TUPE

1. Identify which employees are 'affected employees'. These are employees who – regardless of whether they are likely to transfer or not – may be affected by the transfer or may be affected by measures taken in connection with the transfer.
2. Identify, in respect of each description of affected employee, who are the appropriate representatives of those affected employees. These may be:
   - representatives of an independent trade union recognised by the employer; or (where there is no recognised union)
   - representatives already elected for other purposes who have authority to act in this capacity, bearing in mind the purposes for which they were elected; or
   - representatives elected by the employees for this purpose in an election which the employer must facilitate.
3. The employer has an obligation to inform – and almost certainly also to consult – the 'appropriate representatives' of all affected employees employed by the employer. Define the category of affected employees who are represented by the recognised union. The union representatives will be the appropriate representatives for these purposes. If there are other affected employees who are outside the category of employees in respect of which the union is recognised, consider who the appropriate representatives are for those employees.
4. On the basis that the employer does not recognise a trade union in respect of any given description of affected employee, identify whether there are any appointed/elected employee representatives already in place for other purposes (e.g. a staff council) who it would be appropriate to inform and to consult with in relation to this category of employee. If there are any such representatives already in place, it is the employer's choice whether he deems them to be the appropriate representatives for the purposes of this TUPE information and consultation

---

exercise or whether his employer uses the method in paragraph 5 below to select alternative representatives.

5. If there are no existing representatives identified under paragraph 4 above in respect of a particular description of employee or if the employer would prefer to have new representatives elected (and assuming that the employees concerned are prepared to partici-pate in electing new representatives) an election should be held for the specific purposes of appointing representatives for this TUPE exercise. The following steps should be taken:

   • It is the responsibility of the employer to run the election. The employer must make such arrangements as are 'reason-ably practical' to ensure that the election is fair. Consider how this can best be achieved – make sure that every affected employee has written notice of how the election procedure is to be conducted; give clear instructions as to what candidates need to do to put themselves forward; ensure that the ballot is a secret ballot; take steps to ensure that employees are not concerned about being in any way open to a detriment by reason of participating.

   • The employer must determine how many representatives should be elected. There must be enough to represent all the affected employees, ensuring that there is at least one repre-sentative in respect of each class of employee. A minimum of three to four is advisable. Decide whether the consultation exercise can go ahead as one exercise or whether it is necessary to consult with different categories of employees separately.

   • Determine the term of office of the representatives – ensure that it is long enough to last at least until the transfer has taken place.

   • Candidates must be affected employees. Only affected employees can vote. An employee should have a number of votes equivalent to the number of representatives to be elected (or, where he is a member of a particular class, a number of votes equivalent to the number of representatives to be elected in respect of that particular class).

6. If in respect of a particular description of employee there are no trade unions, no representatives already in place who would be suitable, and the affected employees failed to appoint representa-tives within a 'reasonable time', the employer's obligations are limited to circulating the information which would have been given to the representatives (see paragraph 7 below) to all affected employees in that description of employee. It is difficult

to give guidance on what would be a reasonable time. It should be at least a week and it would be appropriate to point out in the initial circular to employees the time scale within which candidates must come forward.

7. When representatives have been identified, the necessary information should be given to them. This is:
   - the fact that the relevant transfer is to take place, when, approximately, it is to take place and the reasons for it; and
   - the legal, economic and social implications of the transfer for the affected employees; and
   - the measures which the employer envisages it will, in connection with the transfer, take in relation to those employees or, if the employer envisages that no measures will be taken, say so; and
   - the measures which the transferee envisages it will take in connection with the transfer in respect of transferring employees or if none are envisaged say so.

8. The employer should serve a formal request on the transferee asking the transferee to let the employer have the information necessary to enable compliance with the fourth bullet point in 7 above. It has a legal obligation to do so.

9. The information must be given long enough before the transfer to enable consultation between the employer and the appropriate representatives of the affected employees to take place. Consultation is only necessary where measures are envisaged – in the event that no measures are envisaged in respect of affected employees of a particular description, there is no need to consult in relation to those employees and therefore the information may be conveyed only shortly prior to the transfer if the employer chooses to delay. Information must be given in writing. In the case of a union, it must be posted to the address of its head or main office.

10. Consultation must be entered into with a view to seeking the agreement of the representatives to the measures which are proposed. Representations of the representatives must be considered by the employer and a reply must be given, with reasons where the representations are rejected.

An outgoing employer must transfer certain key information relating to the transferring employees to the incoming employer.[21] Save where there are special circumstances, this information must be given not less than 14 days prior to the transfer. There is a continuing duty to update the information once delivered. The box below shows the information which is to be delivered.

Employee liability information
   (a) Identity and age of employee;
   (b) section 1 ERA 1996 particulars;
   (c) information of any:
      (i)   disciplinary procedure taken against an employee;
      (ii) grievance procedure taken by an employee within the previous two years in circumstances where the statutory procedures apply;
   (d) information of any court or tribunal case brought by an employee against the transferor within the previous two years or any claim which the transferor has reasonable grounds to believe the employee may bring against the transferor arising out of the employee's employment with the transferor;
   (e) information regarding any collective agreement which will have effect after the transfer.

9.9. TRANSFER OF TRADE UNION RECOGNITION

Where the undertaking which has been transferred maintains its distinct identity post transfer, then trade union recognition rights are capable of being transferred to the transferee employer. Where an independent trade union is recognised by the transferor employer in respect of employees who become employees of the transferee employer by operation of TUPE, then the transferee employer shall be deemed to have recognised the union to the same extent as recognition was granted by the transferor employer.[22]

9.10. TRANSFER OF COLLECTIVE AGREEMENTS

Collective agreements relating to transferring employees transfer provided that:

   (a) at the time of the transfer, there is a collective agreement in place;
   (b) which has been made by or on behalf of the transferor (that is to say that it would encompass a collective agreement where the transferor participates through a trade association); and
   (c) with a trade union recognised by the transferor in respect of any employee whose contract transfers to the transferee by reason of the application of TUPE.[23]

Where these conditions are satisfied, the collective agreement applies in relation to such employees as if made by the transferee with the union.

9.11. PROTECTION IN A TUPE SITUATION

The prospect of a TUPE transfer brings with it the risk of transferring staff and liabilities which the transferee must accept and plan for (such as pricing in the consequence of higher payroll costs than would be incurred if employees were recruited on the open market) or protection should be sought in the form of an indemnity. While this may be achievable in the context of an acquisition, on a transfer of service providers there will often be no contract between the outgoing and incoming service providers. Hence it becomes necessary for the incoming service provider to look to the client for protection. The client, in turn, should anticipate this situation when drafting the contract for services to ensure that the client and its subsequent sub-contractors are protected against the transfer of liability.

Likewise, if there is no transfer of employees at the end of a contract period, a contractor will be faced with the prospect of significant redundancy liabilities. In these circumstances it is necessary to price in the risk or to lay-off some of the risk by the contract with the client, for example by ensuring that retenders will be made on the basis that all tenderers will be obliged to offer employment on like terms to the employees of the contractor if successful.

9.12. PUBLIC SECTOR OUTSOURCING

TUPE is often encountered within the construction industry in the context of tendering for public sector contracts. In this environment, policy is as important as the law, for instructions have been issued to public sector bodies which prescribe how TUPE should be applied in such circumstances.

The first set of instructions was issued in January 2000 and take the form of a Cabinet Office Statement of Practice 'Staff Transfers in the Public Sector' (COSOP). This was intended to apply to central government departments and agencies and to the NHS (although the policy as it applies to the NHS has subsequently been substantially modified by the Retention of Employment Model, a scheme agreed between the NHS and UNISON which allows staff to opt out of TUPE and to be seconded into the workforce of the private sector contractor whilst retaining employment in the public sector). The Code of Practice on Workforce Matters in Local Authority Service Contracts (the Two Tier Code) introduced in February 2003 extended the application of COSOP to local authority contracting.

A central principle of COSOP is that staff should transfer from the public sector body to the contractor and that TUPE should apply save where there are 'genuinely exceptional reasons' for not doing so. This principle applies not just to the initial contracting out of services but also to subsequent rounds of tendering.

Not only does COSOP seek to promote the transfer of employees, it enhances the terms on which the employees transfer – hence the terminology of 'TUPE plus' terms. Detailed provisions apply to the protection of occupational pensions, redundancy and severance terms. Whereas the transfer of pension rights in relation to occupational schemes under TUPE represents only a partial transfer of employees' rights, COSOP looks for a transfer of broadly equivalent entitlements. Annexed to COSOP is a paper entitled 'A Fair Deal for Staff Pensions', which contains much of the detail.

The ordinary obligations to inform and to consult with appropriate representatives are enhanced.

The Two Tier Code addressed the concern that contractors were seeking to utilise natural turnover in the workforce to reduce terms and conditions of employment and creating a 'two-tier' workforce of those on ex-public sector terms and those on lesser terms. Accordingly, contractors are to be required to recruit replacements for departing staff on terms of employment which are overall no less favourable to the employee than those which applied to the departing employee. In determining what is appropriate, the contractor will be required to consult with employee representatives.

All of these policy requirements are of no direct legal effect, but they represent a codification of what is considered best practice in the public sector and they have legal effect when they are embedded in the terms of the contract for services. As such they will be encountered frequently in public sector contracts and the policies must be considered alongside the law when considering the human resources implications of contracting.

NOTES

1. SI 2006/246
2. 2001/23/EC
3. *Spijkers*
4. *Rygäard*
5. examples as set out in *Spijkers*
6. Regulation 3
7. *Litster* v. *Forth Dry Docks*
8. *Botzen*
9. see *Duncan Web Offset (Maidstone) Ltd* v. *Cooper*
10. Regulation 4(7)
11. *Hay* v. *George Hanson Building Contractors Limited*
12. Regulation 4(9)
13. *Celtec* v. *Astley*
14. Regulation 4(2)
15. *Pall Mall* v. *Bernadone*
16. Regulation 17
17. Regulation 7

18. see *Wilson* v. *St Helens Borough Council*
19. *Berriman* v. *Delabole Slate*
20. under section 98(4) of the Employment Rights Act 1996
21. Regulation 11
22. Regulation 6
23. Regulation 5

CHAPTER 10

Diversity and Public Sector Contracting

Recent years have seen a steady expansion in the scope of discrimination law. All employers must comply with laws which prohibit discrimination on the grounds of sex, race, disability, age, religion or belief and sexual orientation. Consistent with our general approach, we have not set out in this chapter a general explanation of discrimination law as it applies to all employers. However, discrimination law takes on an added dimension in the construction industry in the context of public sector contracting and it is this aspect of discrimination law which is the subject of this chapter for it impacts on how contractors handle diversity issues within their own workforces.

Traditionally, the focus of discrimination law has been to punish employers when discrimination occurs. The law has taken an essentially reactive approach. However, a more proactive approach has been developed as the government has sought to accelerate the pace of changing attitudes in this area. In 2003 the Cabinet Office Strategy Unit published *Ethnic Minorities in the Labour Market*, a report which highlighted the potential role of public procurement in improving equality of employment opportunities. As a consequence, government policy is that comprehensive and clear guidance on equality issues should be given in connection with public procurement.‡ This sits alongside the positive duties which have been imposed on public authorities to take steps to eliminate discrimination and to promote equality of opportunity.[1]

Public authorities are obliged, in carrying out their functions, to have due regard to the need to eliminate discrimination and harassment, to promote equality of opportunity and to promote good relations between different racial groups. Overlaid on these general duties are specific obligations on public authorities which differ across the various categories of discrimination law. For example, the race discrimination laws tend to be more prescriptive than those relating to sex and disability discrimination. Common features are the obligation to prepare an action plan, the collection of data in order to monitor and identify areas of inequality and the taking of steps where any inequality has been identified.

Contractors will ordinarily not be caught directly by these duties on public authorities, as they are not themselves public authorities. However, there may be circumstances in public sector outsourcing where a contractor is exercising a function which would otherwise be exercised by the state, where there is an argument that in so acting the contractor brings itself within the scope of these laws. This is unlikely to be an issue for construction industry employers. Where these laws impact on contractors is in the duties which public authorities impose on contractors when carrying out public sector work.

When putting together a tender specification, the public authority is entitled to take into account 'social issues'. This may be a core requirement (i.e. a mandatory requirement) if the issues are central to the subject of the procurement, resulting in specific provisions in the tender specification and the terms of the contract. For example, a repair and maintenance contract in respect of local authority housing stock would bring the contractor into contact with tenants; this would justify the authority taking steps to accommodate any special needs amongst the tenants.

One impact for contractors arises in relation to the selection of those submitting tenders, whereby the discrimination compliance record of the contractor may be taken into account.

A contractor may be excluded from participating in circumstances where there has been grave performance or misconduct which could include a breach of discrimination law. The public authority must deal with these issues in a proportionate manner (by reference to the significance of diversity issues in the contract as a whole) and focus on remedial measures taken by the contractor to address any problems.

Contractors will be familiar with questioning in tender documentation on these issues, in order to enable public authorities to undertake this aspect of the tender evaluation.

Once successful, the contractor must expect to be made subject, as a matter of contract, to obligations to comply with various non discrimination provisions. Contractors must expect to be monitored in their compliance with these requirements. Non discrimination clauses are typical in standard form contracts. For example, the Commission for Racial Equality (CRE) (which is since 1 October 2007 part of the Equality and Human Rights Commission (EHRC) issued a booklet entitled *Race*

Equality and Public Procurement which sets out, amongst its guidance, a set of standard clauses for insertion into public sector contracts. Public authorities will inevitably be reluctant to depart from such guidance and as a consequence such clauses are likely to be inserted into the contract. Set out below are the standard clauses from the CRE guide:

Model contract clauses

1. Racial discrimination and the promotion of race equality

1.1   The Contractor:

    1.1.1 shall not:

(a) discriminate directly or indirectly, or by way of victimisation or harassment, against any person on grounds of colour, race, nationality, or ethnic or national origins contrary to Part II (Discrimination in the Field of Employment) of the Race Relations Act 1976, as amended (the Act)[2]; and/or

(b) discriminate directly or indirectly or by way of victimisation or harassment against any person on grounds of colour, race, nationality, or ethnic or national origins contrary to Part III of the Act (Discrimination in Other Fields); and/or

(c) contravene Part IV of the Act (Other Unlawful Acts);

where appropriate.[3]

    1.1.2 shall, for purposes of ensuring compliance with sub-clauses 1.1.1 (a) and (c) above, in relation to Contractor Staff[4] employed in the performance of the Agreement,[5] observe as far as possible the provisions of the Commission for Racial Equality's Code of Practice in Employment, as approved by parliament in 1983, [a copy of which is annexed at Schedule [ ]], including, but not limited to, those provisions recommending the adoption, implementation, and monitoring of an equal opportunities policy.

    1.1.3 shall in performing the contract comply with the provisions of section 71(1) of the Act as if the Contractor were a body within the meaning of Schedule 1A to the Act (or any European equivalent which shall be deemed to include without limitation an obligation to have due regard to the need to eliminate unlawful racial discrimination and to promote equality of opportunity and good relations between persons of different racial groups).[6]

1.2   Where in connection with this Agreement the Contractor, its agents or subcontractors, or the Contractor Staff are required to carry out work on the Authority's premises[7] or alongside the Authority's employees on any other premises, the Contractor shall comply with the Authority's own employment policy and codes of practice relating to racial discrimination and equal opportunities, copies of which are annexed at Schedule [ ].[8]

1.3   The Contractor shall:

    1.3.1   monitor the representation among Contractor Staff of persons of different racial groups (which shall mean groups of persons classified as 'ethnic groups' in the most recent official census by the Office of National Statistics or successor body), having regard to the Authority's procedures for monitoring representation among its own employees.

This text is taken, with permission, from *Race Equality and Public Procurement: A guide for public authorities and contractors*, published by the Commission for Racial Equality (CRE) in 2003. The CRE is now part of the new Equality and Human Rights Commission. See www.equalityhumanrights.com for further details.

Contractors should concentrate on the promotion of good practice within their own workforce, to ensure that any competitive disadvantage is removed from the evaluation stage of tendering and to facilitate compliance with contractual obligations where they have been awarded a contract. Suggested areas for particular attention on the part of contractors in this respect are:

- Reviewing policies and employment practices to ensure that appropriate procedures are in place which will meet the standards expected by local authorities.
- Monitoring the contractor's workforce to spot diversity issues and evaluating the quality of that data.
- Compliance with all relevant codes of practice in respect of diversity matters.
- Taking positive action (to the extent permitted by law) to address any inequalities.
- Training the workforce on equality issues so as to promote best practice to reduce the risk of claims.
- Dealing with grievances and tribunal complaints to minimise the claims records.
- Promoting subcontracting opportunities for small firms and ethnic minority businesses.

NOTES

1. See for example the Race Relations (Amendment) Act 2000 which (inter alia) since April 2001 outlaws race discrimination in the functions of public authorities

including procurement, creating a positive duty to promote equality of opportunity and good race relations in carrying out their functions. If a function is outsourced, the authority retains responsibility for the performance of that duty.[*][†]

2. This includes a requirement to comply with section 7 of the Act where this is relevant to the contractor's dealings with sub-contractors.

3. The contractor has a statutory duty to meet these provisions. Most agreements would also include at the end of the agreement a standard clause requiring all parties to observe all statutes and laws in force.

4. 'Contractor Staff' should be defined as all persons employed by the contractor to perform the agreement.

5. As a minimum, it is recommended that this sub-clause should apply to all Contractor Staff. As the CRE's code of practice provides guidance on compliance with the Act in the field of employment, contractors should be encouraged to apply this sub-clause and appropriate race equality policies consistently to the whole of their workforce. It should be recognised, however, that where a contractor employs staff in another member state, compliance with this sub-clause must be in the context of any relevant laws of that state.

6. It is anticipated that this sub-clause will be relevant in an agreement for the provision of services that comprise a function of the authority which the authority has assessed as highly relevant to its compliance with the provisions of section 71(1) of the Act. For example, an agreement to manage a detention centre or a hospital.

7. 'the Authority's premises' should be defined as any premises and land occupied by the Authority for the purposes of carrying out its functions.

8. This clause, which would not normally be suitable in agreements for goods, could be met by the Contractor demonstrating that its employment policy and codes of practice provide race equality protection equivalent to or greater than do those of the Authority. In such circumstances, the Contractor's policies and codes of practice could be annexed to the contract in place of the Authority's.

[*] see also Equality Act 2006 and *Gender equality duty of practice England and Wales*, June 2007 published by the Equal Opportunities Commission, which introduced a gender equality duty from April 2007.

[‡] see also *Transforming government procurement*, HM Treasury; 9 January 2007, and the UK Public Contracts Regulations 2006 which came into force 31 January 2006.

[†] see also *Disability equality duty*, Disability Rights Commission; which from 4 December 2006 introduced a disability equality duty.

Table of Statutes and European Directives

STATUTES

Asylum and Immigration Act 1996

Contracts of Employment and Redundancy Payments Act (Northern Ireland) 1965

Employment Act 1989

Employment Protection (Consolidation) Act 1978

Employment Relations Act 1999

Employment Rights Act 1996

Employment Relations Act 2004

Equality Act 2006

Finance Act 2004

Housing Associations Act 1985

Immigration, Asylum and Nationality Act 2006

Industrial Training Act 1982

National Minimum Wage Act 1998

Pensions Act 2004

Race Relations Act 1976

Race Relations (Amendment) Act 2000

Trade Union and Labour Relations (Consolidation) Act 1992

Trade Union Reform and Employment Rights Act 1993

EUROPEAN DIRECTIVES

Acquired Rights Directive (Council Directive 77/187/EEC)

Working Time Directive (Council Directive 93/104/EC, 2003/88/EC)

Young Workers' Directive (Council Directive 94/33/EC)

Table of statutory instruments and orders

Table of cases

AD Bly Construction Ltd v. *Cochrane* 23.11.05 EAT 0243/05

Ainsworth v. *IRL* [2005] ICR 1149, [2005] IRLR 465

Bacica v. *Muir* [2006] IRLR 35

Barber & Others v. *RJB Mining (UK) Ltd* [1999] IRLR 308, HCQB

Beckmann v. *Dynamco Whicheloe Macfarlane* [2002] All ER (EC) 865; [2002] ECR I-4893; [2002] 2 CMLR 45; [2002] CEC 547; [2003] ICR 50; [2002] IRLR 578; [2002] Emp LR 970; [2002] OPLR 289; [2002] Pens. LR 287; Times, June 17, 2002

Berriman v. *Delabole Slate Ltd* [1985] ICR 546, [1985] IRLR 305

Botzen Rotterdamsche Droogdok Maatschappij BV (C-186/83) [1986] 2 CMLR 50, ECJ

Byrne Brothers (Formwork) Ltd v. *Baird* [2002] ICR 667; [2002] IRLR 96; [2002] Emp. LR 567

Carmichael v. *National Power plc* [1999] ICR 1226 HL

Cassidy v. *Ministry of Health* [1951] 2 KB 343, [1951] 1 All ER 574

Celtec v. *Astley* [2006] UKHL 29; [2006] 1 WLR 2420; [2006] 4 All ER 27; [2006] ICR 992; [2006] IRLR 635; (2006) 156 NLJ 1061; (2006) 150 SJLB 856; Times, June 23, 2006

Cotswold Developments Construction Limited v. *Williams* [2006] IRLR 181

Duncan Web Offset (Maidstone) Ltd v. *Cooper* [1995] IRLR 633, EAT

Express & Echo Publications Ltd v. *Tanton* [1999] IRLR 367, [1999] ICR 693, CA

Filcom Ltd v. *Ross* 31.1.95 EAT 472/93

Hall (HM Inspector of Taxes) v. *Lorimer* [1994] IRLR 171, [1994] ICR 218 CA, [1994] 1 All ER 250

Hay v. *George Hanson (Building Contractors) Ltd* [1986] IRLR 427, EAT

James v. *Greenwich Council* [2007] ICR 577; [2007] IRLR 168

Kigass Acro Components Ltd v. *Brown* [2002] ILR 697, [2002] IRLR 312

Lane v. *Shire Roofing (Oxford) Ltd* [1995] IRLR 493

Lee v. *Chung and Shun Shing Construction and Engineering Co. Ltd* [1990] 2 AC 374, [1990] 2 WLR 1173, [1990] ICR 409, [1990] IRLR 236

Litster v. *Forth Dry Docks & Engineering Co. Ltd* [1990] 1 AC 546, [1989] 2WLR 634, [1989] 1 All ER 1134, [1989] ICR 341, [1989] IRLR 161, HL

Marshalls Clay Products Ltd v. *Caulfield* [2004] ICR 436

Martin v. *South Bank University* [2003] ECR I-12859; [2004] 1 CMLR 15; [2004] CEC 90; [2004] ICR 1234; [2004] IRLR 74; [2003] OPLR 317; [2003] Pens. LR 329

Market Investigations Ltd v. *Minister of Social Security* [1969] 2 QB 173, [1969] 2 WLR 1, [1968] 3 All ER 732

North Wales Probation Area v. *Edwards* 12.12.2007 EAT 468/07

O'Kelly v. *Trusthouse Forte plc* [1984] QB 90, [1983] 3 WLR 605, [1983] ICR 728, [1983] 3 All ER 456, [1983] IRLR 369

Pall Mall v. *Bernadone* [1999] IRLR 617, QBD

R. v. *Attorney General for Northern Ireland ex parte Burns* [1999] IRLR 315

R (on the application of the Broadcasting, Entertainment, Cinematographic & Theatre Union) v. *Secretary of State for Trade and Industry* C-173/99 (BECTU) [2001] IRLR 559

Ready-Mixed Concrete (South East Ltd) v. *Minister of Pensions and National Insurance* [1968] 2 QB 497, [1968] 2 WLR 775, [1968] 1 All ER 433

Real Time Civil Engineering Limited v. *Callaghan* [2005] WL 3719519

Rygaard v. *Stro Molle Akustik* (C-48/94) A/S, [1996] IRLR 51

Specialeyes (Optical Services) Ltd Re. Taxation, 4 July 1991

Spijkers v. *Gebroeders Benedik Abbatoir* [1986] 3 ECR 1119, ECJ

Staffordshire Sentinel Newspapers Limited v. *Potter* [2004] I.R.L.R. 752

Stevenson Jordan & Harrison v. *McDonnell & Evans* [1952] 1 TLR 101, CA

Transmontana Coach Distributors Ltd v. *Walker* 16.6.95 EAT 74/95

Wall & Others v. *Standard Telephones & Cables Ltd* [1991] IRLR 286 QBD

Wilson v. *St Helens Borough Council* [1998] WLR 1070, [1998] IRLR 706, HL

Useful sources

ACAS	www.acas.org.uk
B&CE	www.bandce.org.uk
Border and Immigration Agency	www.ind.homeoffice.gov.uk
Building Magazine	www.building-focus.co.uk
CBI	www.cbi.org.uk
CITB	www.citb.org.uk
Civil Engineering Contractors' Association	www.ceca.co.uk
Construction Federation	www.constructionconfederation.co.uk
Construction Industry Board	www.ciboard.org.uk
Construction News	www.cnplus.co.uk
Department for Business, Enterprise and Regulatory Reform	www.berr.gov.uk
Electrical Contractors' Association	www.eca.co.uk
Engineering Construction Industry Training Board	www.ecitb.org.uk
Equality and Human Rights Commission (EHRC)	www.equalityhumanrights.com
European Union	europe.eu.int
GMB	www.gmb.org.uk
Health and Safety Executive	www.hse.gov.uk

Heating and Ventilation Contractors' Association	www.hvca.org.uk
HM Revenue and Customs	www.hmrc.gov.uk
HM Treasury	www.hm-treasury.gov.uk
Institution of Civil Engineers	www.ice.org.uk
Joint Industry Board for the Electrical Contracting Industry	www.jib.org.uk
National Federation of Builders	www.builders.org.uk
Parliament	www.parliament.uk/
Pinsent Masons	www.pinsentmasons.com
Royal Institute of Chartered Surveyors	www.rics.org.uk
Society of Construction Law	www.scl.org.uk
TGWU	www.tgwu.org.uk
Thomas Telford	www.thomastelford.com
Trade Union Congress (TUC)	www.tuc.org.uk
UCATT	www.ucatt.org.uk
Unite	www.amicustheunion.org

Bibliography and further reading

Her Majesty's Revenue and Customs. Factsheet CIS340: *Guide for contractors and subcontractors*. Available on-line at www.hmrc.gov.uk/new-cis/detailed-guidance.htm

Her Majesty's Revenue and Customs. Factsheet CIS341: *A quick guide to the new Construction Industry Scheme*. Available on-line at www.hmrc.gov.uk/new-cis/detailed-guidance.htm

Her Majesty's Revenue and Customs. Factsheet CIS342: *Registering for new CIS – advice for subcontractors*. Available on-line at www.hmrc.gov.uk/new-cis/detailed-guidance.htm

Her Majesty's Revenue and Customs. Fact sheet CIS343: *Applying to be paid gross – advice for subcontractors*. Available on-line at www.hmrc.gov.uk/new-cis/detailed-guidance.htm

Her Majesty's Revenue and Customs. Factsheet CIS344: *Getting paid by a contractor – advice for subcontractors*. Available on-line at www.hmrc.gov.uk/new-cis/detailed-guidance.htm

Her Majesty's Revenue and Customs. Factsheet CIS345: *Verifying a subcontractor – advice for contractors*. Available on-line at www.hmrc.gov.uk/new-cis/detailed-guidance.htm

Her Majesty's Revenue and Customs. Factsheet CIS346: *The monthly return – advice for contractors*. Available on-line at www.hmrc.gov.uk/new-cis/detailed-guidance.htm

Her Majesty's Revenue and Customs. Factsheet CIS347: *A contractor's obligations – advice for contractors*. Available on-line at www.hmrc.gov.uk/new-cis/detailed-guidance.htm

Her Majesty's Revenue and Customs. Factsheet *CIS348: The scope of the Scheme – a quick guide.* Available on-line at www.hmrc.gov.uk/new-cis/detailed-guidance.htm

Her Majesty's Revenue and Customs. Factsheet CIS349: *Are your workers employed or self-employed? – advice for contractors.* Available on-line at www.hmrc.gov.uk/new-cis/detailed-guidance.htm

Her Majesty's Revenue and Customs. Factsheet CIS359: *The new Construction Industry Scheme – a quick guide for agents.* Available on-line at www.hmrc.gov.uk/new-cis/detailed-guidance.htm

McMullen, J. *Business Transfers and Employee Rights.* Butterworths, 1998, London

Wallington, P. *Butterworths Employment Law Handbook*; 5th edition. Butterworths, 2007, London

Upex, R. and Shrubsall, V. *Contracts of Employment: Law & Practice.* FT Law & Tax, 1997, London

Countering Avoidance in the Provision of Personal Services. 2000, IR35, HM Revenue and Customs, London

Howard, G. *Drafting Contracts of Employment.* The Law Society, 2004, The Law Society, London

Brearley, K. and Selwyn, B. *Employment Covenants and Confidential Information: Law, Practice and Technic*, 3rd edition; Tottel, (due Summer) 2008, London

Slade, E. *Employment Handbook*, 21st edition; Tolleys Employment Service, 2007, London

Ryley, M. *Employment Law Aspects of Mergers and Acquisitions: A Practical Guide*, 2nd edition; Thorogood, 2006, London

Jordans/Chartered Institute of Personnel and Development, *Employment Law Service,* 1998 and updates, Jordans, Bristol

Harvey on Industrial Relations and Employment Law, Butterworths, 2000 and updates, London

Upex, R. and Ryley, M. *TUPE: Law & Practice*, Jordans, 2006, Jordans, Bristol

Freedland, M. The Personal Employment Contract, Oxford, 2006, Oxford University Press, Oxford

Edwards, M. and Malone, M. *Tolley's Equal Opportunities Handbook*; 2nd edition Tolley, London

MacDonald, I. *Immigration Law and Practice in the UK*; 6th edition, Butterworths, 2005, London

Index

Page numbers in *italics* refer to Figures.